23996

DATE DUE

APR 3 0 1985			
MAY 1 6 1989			
NOV 2 1993			
OCT 2 7			

Ellis, R. Hobart
Knowing the atomic nucleus.

Knowing the Atomic Nucleus

R. Hobart Ellis, Jr.

Knowing the Atomic Nucleus

Lothrop, Lee & Shepard Company

New York

Diagrams by Susan Stan

Library of Congress Cataloging in Publication Data

Ellis, R   Hobart.
  Knowing the atomic nucleus.

  SUMMARY: Describes the discovery, nature, and potential of the atomic nucleus,
with explanations of atomic structure and behavior, radioactivity, fission, and fusion.
    1. Nuclear physics—Juvenile literature. 2. Atoms—Juvenile literature. [1. Nu-
clear physics. 2. Atoms] I. Title.

QC173.E42   539.7   72-11985

ISBN 0-688-41295-5
ISBN 0-688-51295-X (lib. bdg.)

For S. T. S., faithful reader,
and S. D. E., devoted collaborator

Contents

Knowing the Atomic Nucleus

· (1) ·

Why a Nucleus?
What Does It Do?

The idea of an atom is very old—at least as old as the Greeks and Romans, who wrote about it more than two thousand years ago. But the thought of an atom with a nucleus is quite new. Only in 1911 did the British scientist Ernest Rutherford discover that the atom is built around a tiny dense core at the center, which we now call the nucleus. It may seem strange that so long a time passed between the first talk of the atom and the first suggestion of what we call the nuclear atom.

Perhaps the explanation is the naturalness of one idea and the surprising nature of the other. After all, if you start to divide a substance into smaller and smaller pieces, only two real possibilities are available. Either you can continue without limit to cut and divide, every smaller piece being like the bigger ones, or else you come to an end. You get to a smallest piece that you cannot cut any smaller. That is the meaning of the ancient word atom. The word has a somewhat different meaning now, but originally it was the piece so small that it could not be cut smaller.

For a long time both of these ideas had people who believed in them. Some people thought that when things are cut small

11

enough, the smallest pieces must be atoms; some thought that the cutting could go on and on forever, no matter how small the pieces became. But chemists in the last century became quite thoroughly convinced that atoms exist.

The first evidence came from the way substances combine in chemical reactions. In such processes two or more substances become one, or one substance separates to make two or more. A simple example is the burning of paper, in which carbon and hydrogen of the paper combine with oxygen of the air to make smoke and ash.

Chemists found that in chemical reactions simple substances join in exact proportions. For example, oxygen and the lightweight gas hydrogen can be made to combine chemically. The combination is the familiar compound water. The interesting fact is that whenever these two gases join to form water, they do so in a very definite proportion—about eight parts by weight of oxygen to one part of hydrogen. If a larger proportion of hydrogen is present, the extra amount will be left over after the change takes place. If there is a larger proportion of oxygen, some of it will be left afterward.

The reason is that two hydrogen atoms become linked to each atom of oxygen, and each oxygen atom weighs sixteen times what each hydrogen atom weighs. The result is a water molecule (written H_2O), in which the oxygen weighs eight times as much as the hydrogen.

The water molecule has one oxygen atom and two hydrogen atoms.

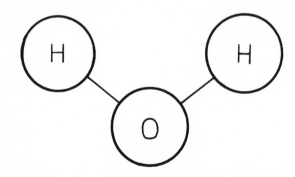

Why a Nucleus? What Does It Do?

The chemists found still more evidence of atoms. By studying the amounts of elements that went into simple compounds, they found they could figure out the weights of the atoms. Study of different reactions—hydrogen with oxygen, oxygen with carbon, carbon with sulfur, and so on—made it possible to assign weights to all the atoms, presuming they existed.

After discovering what we now call the atomic weights, the chemists started making lists of the chemical elements in order of their weights. They found that how an element behaved depended on where it fell in the list.

Evidence like this convinced scientists that atoms really exist, that each of the chemical elements—hydrogen, oxygen, zinc, lead and all the others—is made of atoms that are all alike and that many other common substances like water and table salt are made of atoms in combinations. So they started to think about what the atoms look like.

They had one other bit of evidence that was important in imagining a picture or, as scientists say, making a model of an atom. In experiments with electricity they had found that electric currents can cause chemical changes. Moreover they had discovered what they called the electron—the smallest amount of electricity that could cause any chemical change at all. Later this electron turned out to be one of the fundamental particles that make up atoms.

So they felt that the atom was in some way made up of electric parts, and their first model of the atom was the "plum-pudding" atom. Electrons, which were known to have a negative charge, were thought to be stuffed into a lump of the other kind of charge (positive) like plums in a pudding. Because the two kinds of charge were of the same size, equal amounts of both kinds of charge were in an atom; the two canceled each other, and the whole atom seemed to have no charge at all.

Scientists worked with this plum-pudding model and made many calculations about it. Then Ernest Rutherford came along with an experiment that upset the pudding. Rutherford was for many years a professor of physics at Cambridge University in England and was, by a wide margin, the man who did the most to develop an understanding of the nucleus. His experiment showed that the pudding atom would not do—that instead one must believe in the nuclear atom, which is the model we accept now.

Very briefly, Rutherford's experiment consisted of shooting a beam of electrically charged particles at gold foil and seeing how they went through it. By experimenting, Rutherford had already found out that radioactive materials shot out charged particles. So he put a little of a radioactive element into a small metal tube. Then only the particles that went along the tube could get out, so that he had a little gun shooting all its particles in one direction.

"Bullets" from the gun came out fast, and Rutherford could make gold foil very thin—so thin that particles from the sun could go right through. If the atoms in gold were puddings, Rutherford would have seen his particles go right through the foil without very much deflection. But he found a different behavior. Many particles did, indeed, go straight through, but some bounced off at all angles—even in the direction they came from.

The Rutherford experiment. Some particles were widely deflected; some even bounced back.

radioactive material

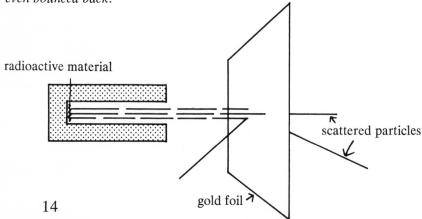

scattered particles

gold foil ↗

Why a Nucleus? What Does It Do?

It was as if someone threw baseballs at a bag of feathers, and suddenly one of the balls bounced straight back to the thrower. He would know that something in the bag was denser and harder than feathers.

Of course Rutherford thought about what his experiment meant. He could tell how many particles his little gun was shooting out each second, how many went straight through his foil, how many bounced off at large angles, and how many bounced back from the foil. From all of this evidence he could figure out that something in the atom must be very small and very heavy. Moreover he could tell that this small, heavy object must have an electric charge, and he could figure out just how big the object must be. This tiny, dense charged object he called the nucleus—a word meaning core or kernel or seed.

It is hard to talk about atomic and nuclear sizes. Atoms are incredibly small. It takes more than a thousand million million million atoms to make up the drop of water that falls from a medicine dropper, but there really is no good way to grasp the significance of such figures.

Moreover, beyond this incredible smallness is the vast range of sizes in the parts of an atom. A car, which you can measure by stretching out your arms and taking a couple of steps, is made up of parts that you can pick up with your hands and fingers. But if the atom were the size of the car, its nucleus would be so small that you could hardly see it, let alone handle it. And the nucleus is made up of pieces smaller still.

If the atom were enlarged until the nucleus was the size of a grape seed and if all parts were kept in the same proportions during the enlargement, the radius of the blown-up atom would be about the length of a football field. In other words, if you stood at the corner of a football field holding the grape-seed-size nucleus on the tip of your finger, the outside edge of the atom would be near the opposite corner of the field about three hundred feet or a hundred yards or a hundred meters away. The

15

The nuclear atom—a dense and heavy central core surrounded by an electron cloud.

grape-seed nucleus is at the center. Arranged around it in a big ball are all of the electrons, and the distance from the nucleus to the outer edge of the ball is the length of the football field.

Sometimes it is useful to picture the electrons, which form all of the atom outside the nucleus, as if they were going around the nucleus the way the earth and the other planets go around the sun. This is a simplified view; it is more accurate to say that the rest of the atom is occupied by the electrons. They spread out in various cloudlike patterns, and they are held in place by electric forces between themselves and the tiny nucleus at the center.

16

Why a Nucleus? What Does It Do?

The nucleus contains no electrons, however. It is made up of just two kinds of particles. They are called "protons" and "neutrons," and the two are much alike. Depending on what kind of an atom it is, there may be as few as one of these particles in the nucleus or as many as about two hundred and forty. The number of protons in an atom is about the same as the number of neutrons.

To find out about things as small as an atom and its pieces is no easy job. You can't just pull an atom apart to see what makes it behave as it does, the way you could take apart an alarm clock. But thanks to his endless curiosity man has found out, and continues to find out, more and more.

As you could peel an orange to find out what is inside, man has explored the atom from the outside in. Now we can use what we know to see how an atom is built, working from the inside out and starting with the pieces that go together to make it.

·(2)·

The Three Building Blocks

A surprising thing about an atom is the small number of kinds of pieces that make it up. Start with any atom in the universe. Take it apart until you come to the fundamental parts. When you get through, you will have only three kinds of pieces. These particles, as they are called, are protons, neutrons, and electrons. All protons are exactly alike; all neutrons are exactly alike; all electrons are exactly alike. There are no big and small protons as there are big and small red apples.

The most important things to know about any particle are its mass and electric charge.

The mass of any object is the amount of material in it. We

Three kinds of particles—protons, electrons, neutrons—make up all atoms.

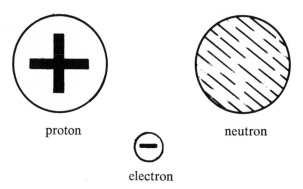

proton   neutron

electron

speak, for example, of a pound of sugar or iron. In everyday terms the amount of mass in any object corresponds to its weight.

It's not always easy, though, to use weight to tell how much mass anything has. How could you weigh a pound of air, for instance? It just floats in the air around it. Besides, anything that weighs a pound at sea level weighs less at the top of a mountain. The weight of an object is the attraction exerted on it by the earth, and that pull, which we call gravity, becomes less as the distance between the object and the center of the earth gets larger.

A better way to define and measure the mass of any object is to see how quickly it moves when pushes and pulls are applied to it. As an example, suppose ten pool balls lie on a pool table and among them are ten light rubber balls of the same size. Suppose that they are all painted alike and that in a dim light they all look alike. Yet you can tell which balls are ivory and which ones are rubber by pushing each one with a cue stick. The rubber balls, having less mass, will move easily, and the massive ivory balls will be harder to move. An object with more mass is more resistant to a force than one with less mass. All of the elementary particles, as we call electrons, protons, and neutrons, have mass.

Two of the particles, the proton and the electron, also have electric charge. This, too, is an everyday concept, but it is not quite as everyday as mass. We often experience its effects in static electricity, which is really electric charge that is trapped, standing still, not moving as it does when it forms an electric current. It shows itself in several ways. If you scuff your feet on the rug and then see a spark jump from your finger to a light switch, a static charge has jumped from your finger to the switch. If you pull a comb through your hair and then hold it in a beam of sunlight, some dust particles in the beam are attracted to the comb, and others are pushed away. Forces between charges on the comb and charges on the dust particles do the pushing and pulling. A plastic jacket pulled from a phonograph record is often attracted to the record by the charges both have acquired, and at the same time the jacket may push away another jacket similarly charged. One can talk about electric charges mainly in terms of these forces that exist among them.

There are two kinds of charges, and they are called, for convenience, positive and negative. The forces that act between any two charges are described by very simple laws. Any two charges of like sign—that is, two positive charges or two negative charges—push each other apart (scientists say they "repel" each other). Any two unlike charges—a positive and a negative —attract each other. And the amount of force, whether it is a repulsion or an attraction, becomes greater as the charges come closer together. These laws are universal, which means that they are true about any two similar charges anywhere.

One cannot pick up two charges as one can pick up two tennis balls, move them around, and observe the forces between them. Other experiments are possible, though. Scientists can cause two charged particles to pass each other, and they can observe whether one of them causes the path of the other one to bend.

Whenever two positively charged objects are held up and brought together, a force acts to push them apart; that is, they repel each other. Moreover as the two charges come closer together, the force gets stronger as the distance becomes smaller. When the distance becomes half as great, the force becomes four times as great. If the distance is reduced to a quarter of the original amount, the force becomes sixteen times what it was originally. The mathematician's way of expressing this is, "Two positive charges repel each other with a force that is inversely proportional to the square of the distance between them."

An experiment with two negative charges will show the same result. They will repel each other, and the force will become greater when the distance between them becomes smaller. Here, too, the force will be four times as great for half the distance, sixteen times as great for a quarter of the distance, and so on.

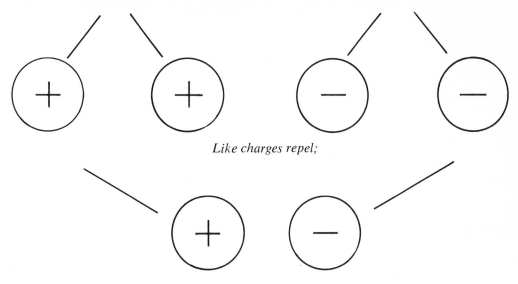

Like charges repel;

unlike charges attract.

On the other hand if a positive charge is near a negative one, they will attract each other; that is, each one will pull on the other. As they come closer, the force of attraction will increase in the same way that the force of repulsion did.

There is one more way to increase the force between any two charges, and that is to increase the amount of one or both of the charges. Without changing the distance between two charges, the experimenter might double one of them. If he adds another charge of the same size and kind to the charge on the left, the two together will push or pull on the charge at the right with double force.

There is a way to measure the amount of a charge. It is to measure the force exerted on any charge at a given location. If a new charge is put in the same spot and the new force is measured, the new force indicates the amount of the new charge. Twice as much force means twice as much charge. This method also shows whether the new charge is positive or negative. If the original force was a push, and the new force is also a push, the new charge must be of the same kind as the original one. If the force changes from a push to a pull, the new charge must be different; it is the kind that is opposite from the original.

Each of the basic building blocks, the atomic particles, has a mass. The proton has positive charge, the electron has negative charge, and the neutron has no charge at all.

Because conceiving of such tiny particles is difficult, it will be convenient to imagine them tremendously enlarged. If the proton were a hundred million million times as large in diameter as it really is, it would be about the size of a grapefruit; let us say that a yellow grapefruit indicates the proton.

The neutron is a tiny bit larger than a proton. Let us say that a grapefruit ripened into a darker color stands for the neutron. The electron is much less massive than either. Its mass is about 1/1800 that of the proton; that is to say, if you take 1800 electrons together, the total mass is about that of a single proton. A little green pea could represent an electron on the same scale that makes yellow and dark grapefruit appropriate for the other two particles.

Because the electron is the smallest of the three particles, it is convenient to use the electron mass as a unit. In other words, you can say that the electron has a mass of one and then measure all other masses in terms of this electron mass.

Besides having mass, the electron also has an electric charge of a definite amount. This charge can serve as the unit of charge. The reason is that all charges come in amounts that are one, two, two thousand, or some other whole number times the amount of the electron charge. No one has ever observed half or two thirds or one and a half times an electron charge.

The electron has a negative charge. However, all positive charges come in units of this same amount. So the unit of positive charge is just as big as the unit of negative charge although the charges are of opposite kind.

All electrons are exactly alike. That is why it makes sense to speak of the electron mass as a unit of mass and the electron charge as a unit of charge. Every electron has exactly the same negative charge and exactly the same mass as every other electron.

The Three Building Blocks

The proton, too, has an electric charge. The charge is positive, and it is of just the same amount as the charge of the electron even though the proton has 1800 times as much mass as the electron.

When we speak of whether a charge is positive or negative, we say we are talking about the "sign" of the charge. A negative sign stands for the electron charge and all others of the same kind; a positive sign stands for the other kind of charge—the kind that belongs to the proton.

The third fundamental particle, the neutron, has no electric charge. In other words, if it comes into the neighborhood of a proton or electron, no electric force will be exerted between the neutron and the other particle. So we call it a neutral particle, meaning it has no charge, and it is properly named neutron.

Because the neutron has no electric charge, it was the last of the three basic building blocks to be discovered. Most of the actions by which particles make themselves known and cause the effects they do are associated with the electric forces they exert on one another. But the neutron goes where charged particles cannot go and leaves no trace of itself. So for a long time nobody knew it existed.

Yet although no electric force acts between the neutron and either an electron or a proton, another force does affect it. It acts only among neutrons and protons and only when two of them are very close together, as in a nucleus. It is a force of attraction, and it acts between any pair of these particles whether they are two protons, two neutrons, or one of each. Called the nuclear force, it acts like a layer of glue on the surface of the particles. Imagine our yellow and dark grapefruits all smeared with honey.

But the nuclear force acts only among a very small number of particles. This is a bit like saying that if our yellow and dark grapefruits have honey on them, one grapefruit can be stuck to only a small number of others. Once it is covered, more grapefruits cannot come close enough to stick to it.

23

The nuclear force is quite different from the electric forces we talked about earlier. Electric forces act at all distances and among any number of charged particles. On the other hand, the nuclear force acts only on protons and neutrons, and it acts only when they are very, very close together.

The models we are using are very simple ones, and they cannot really show all properties of the particles. They are useful in giving some ideas of how the masses and charges compare.

But if the models are simple, so are the basic facts about our three basic building blocks, the three elementary particles. The electron has negative charge and a mass that never changes. The proton has about 1800 times as much mass and a positive charge equal in amount to that of the electron. The neutron has no charge at all and just a little more mass than the proton.

·(**3**)·

The Pieces Fit Together

Some believe that our universe started with a big bang. Out of the explosion came protons, neutrons, and electrons in great numbers, and with them large quantities of radiation— heat and light. Then particles began to bump into each other and form combinations. Combinations made bigger combinations until the atoms we know today had been formed. Atoms joined to form molecules, stars, planets, and living things.

This is not the only possibility for our origin. Some scientists believe in quite different theories. Whether the big-bang theory is right or not, though, it illustrates an important fact. If enough neutrons, protons, and electrons were thrown together somehow, they would form combinations, and the combinations would be atoms. These atoms would be just like those that make up everything around us—water, air, wood, metal—and also you and me.

Of all these atoms the simplest is hydrogen. At its center is a single proton. Combined with it in a hydrogen atom is one electron, tinier still. When these two particles, proton and electron, combine to form a hydrogen atom, they fill a space that is huge compared with the dimensions we associate with either particle alone. On the grapefruit-and-pea scale, the atom would be about five miles across.

25

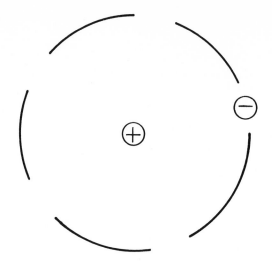

The hydrogen atom—one proton with one electron.

When scientists first began to discover the structure of the atom, they thought that the proton sat at the center and the electron whirled around it like a planet around a sun. In terms of our blown-up model, the little green pea would whirl around the yellow grapefruit in a circle about five miles in diameter. More recently the view has changed. Now the electron is believed to occupy all of the space outside the proton. So we can think of the electron made into a thin pea soup and spread throughout a big sphere with the grapefruit in the middle.

Such a picture represents a hydrogen atom at rest or, as scientists say, "in the ground state." Sometimes, though, a hydrogen atom is disturbed. In a flame, for example, two hydrogen atoms might bump into each other.

In such a disturbance the electron, which extends so very far out into space from the central proton, is usually the part that is affected. It can be bumped into shapes and sizes that are quite different from the ground state. Surprisingly, though, it cannot take just any shape. Certain very distinct ones are available to it as if certain gelatin molds existed in space and the electron had to fit into one or another of these molds. Each of the molds is called a state.

The electron in an atom can move from state to state as a marble can move on a flight of stairs. The marble can fall easily from step to step toward the bottom, and something has to lift it if it is to move up. The electron can fall from state to state as it moves closer to the proton in the nucleus, to which it is drawn electrically. But something has to lift it if it is to move from a state near the nucleus to another that is farther out.

Because electrons in atoms act somewhat like marbles on a flight of stairs, we say that an electron moving from a state farther out to one that is closer to the nucleus is "falling to a lower state." And electrons moving away from the nucleus are "being lifted into higher states."

Moving an electron to a higher state is something like blowing up a balloon. To make the balloon bigger, you have to blow in air against the pressure of the air already there. To make an electron move out and be farther away from the nucleus that attracts it, something has to push. The push can come from a collision with another atom or particle, or from a flash of light.

Besides jumping to higher or lower states, the electron of a hydrogen atom has another way to change its own shape. A change can occur when the hydrogen atom joins with one or more other atoms. Such a combination is a molecule, and this is the smallest piece of any substance that can exist by itself. For example, water is made of hydrogen and oxygen. An oxygen atom is bigger than a hydrogen atom. It has eight protons in its nucleus at its center, about eight neutrons there also (sometimes one or two more or less) and eight electrons around the outside. When two hydrogen atoms join an oxygen atom to make a water molecule, the electrons mix, and the mixing ties the atoms together.

When things like this happen to the hydrogen atom, though, the proton remains essentially undisturbed at the center. The

27

electron jumps from state to state, bumps into other particles, and mixes with other electrons to form bonds between atoms. But the yellow grapefruit center of our blown-up model, more than two miles away from the edge of the atom where all the action is, remains nicely isolated and protected.

Only the hydrogen atom, though, is so simple as to have only one particle in the nucleus and only two particles altogether. All other elements of our universe are made of atoms in which the nuclei have more than one proton. In fact the number of protons in the nucleus tells us what the element is, and all elements can be made by starting with a hydrogen atom and adding protons, one by one, to the nucleus.

That is, they could be made in this way if we could pick up protons and neutrons like grapefruits and stick them together one at a time. Of course we can't really do it unless we have a machine in a laboratory that shoots protons into atoms where they can stick to make new kinds of nuclei. But just to make talking about atoms easier I will talk as if we could add and subtract protons and neutrons, like grapefruit, one at a time.

One proton, as we have seen, makes a hydrogen nucleus. If

By adding protons and electrons we "make" the bigger atoms.

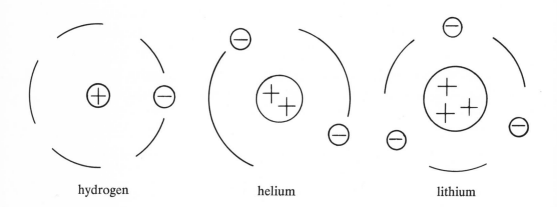

hydrogen   helium   lithium

28

one proton is added so that the nucleus has two, the nucleus is that of helium, which is atom number two. Three protons make a lithium nucleus, and lithium is atom number three.

Suppose, then, that we can add protons one by one, starting with hydrogen, until all the numbers from one to ninety-two are occupied. The ninety-two kinds of atoms then represent all of the chemical elements: hydrogen, helium, lithium, beryllium (4), boron (5), carbon (6), nitrogen (7), oxygen (8), aluminum (13), chromium (24), iron (26), copper (29), silver (47), tin (50), platinum (78), gold (79), lead (82) and so on. All of the ninety-two elements that occur in nature are listed on pages 35–36.

As protons are added to make the nuclei of heavier atoms, other changes take place also. Perhaps the most important one is that heavier atoms have more electrons. Each has, in fact, the same number of electrons in the space outside the nucleus as the number of protons in the nucleus.

There is a simple reason for this. If the number of electrons is different from the number of protons in any atom, that atom has a left-over electric charge of one kind or the other. Then it loses or gains electrons until the numbers are equal. Suppose, for example, that an atom of copper with 29 protons in its nucleus is floating around somewhere with only 28 electrons. Somewhere there will be a free electron, because electrons on the outer edges of atoms are not held very tightly. An accidental hit or knock or vibration is always jarring one or two loose.

A free electron near our copper atom will be pulled in by the 29 protons and pushed away by 28 electrons. The pull will be greater than the push. So the electron moves in and joins the atom. Then the atom has the same number of both kinds of particles. It is electrically neutral and does not attract any more electrons.

In the same way, if an atom has too many electrons, all of them push each other away harder than the smaller number of

29

protons attracts them. As a result, extra electrons are lost until the numbers are equal and everything is in balance.

The electrons around a bigger nucleus behave like the electron of a hydrogen atom. There are molds into which they can fit, or, in more scientific language, they occupy certain states like the different states that the electron of a hydrogen atom can occupy. Because there are many of them, though, matters are more complicated, and different rules apply in an atom that has many protons in its nucleus. The first and most important rule is that only one electron at a time can occupy a state. The rule is like one that applies to wives in families. One wife is all right, but two wives are one too many.

Around any nucleus are many states, like gelatin molds. They are arranged in a pattern as fine and precise as the one in a well-knitted sweater, and the ones nearest to the nucleus are usually filled first.

One can imagine, for example, a nucleus of an oxygen atom with all electrons removed. The nucleus might stand somewhere in space with no electrons anywhere around. As electrons came along, they would join the atom one at a time.

The first added electron would occupy a state quite near the nucleus. Then when a second electron was added it would occupy another state, also quite near the nucleus but different from the first.

When a third electron was added it would find that states one and two were occupied and that state number three was not near the first two. It would be farther out from the nucleus. Thus the first two electrons in an oxygen atom do in fact occupy what is called a "closed shell." Their places are very close to the center of the atom. Then electrons three, four, five, six, seven and eight occupy a set of states in another shell a bit farther out from the nucleus than the first shell.

When we have still bigger atoms, for example iron with 26 electrons, we find that the first two occupy the first shell and

30

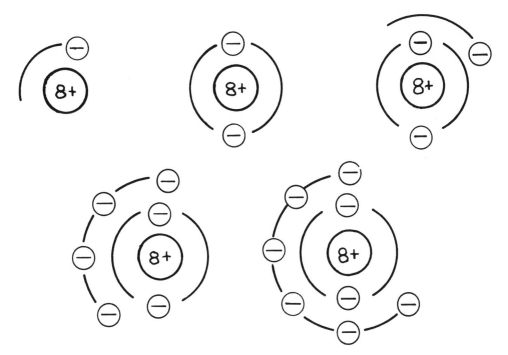

Adding electrons to make an oxygen atom. Each additional electron must occupy a new and different place or "state."

fill it. The next shell has states for eight more electrons, and eight make it filled, or closed. Eight more close a third shell, and so on until the atom has as many electrons as protons.

Atoms join together to make molecules. The atoms that make up any molecule are held together by some combination of their electrons. The outermost electrons usually take part in the bonding; the ones in inner closed shells are left almost undisturbed when two atoms meet, join, and form a molecule.

An example of a molecule made from larger atoms is sodium chloride, common table salt. The sodium atom has 11 electrons, two in an inner closed shell, eight in an outer closed shell, and a single electron that is outside in a third shell. The chlorine atom has 17 electrons, two in an inner shell, eight in the second shell, and seven in the third shell. The outermost shell would be closed if it had one more electron; it has a space for one more electron than the atom possesses. When sodium and chlorine

31

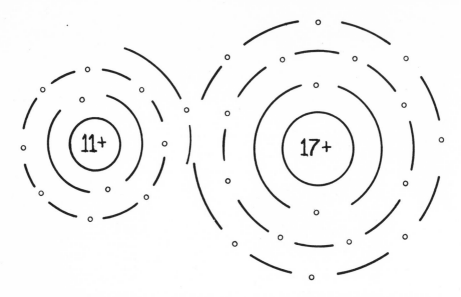

A sodium atom and a chlorine atom join chemically to make sodium chloride—table salt.

atoms combine to make a sodium chloride molecule, the outermost electron of sodium fits into the hole that is left in the outermost shell of chlorine, and the two atoms share this single electron. The electron shared between the atoms forms the glue that keeps them together in the molecule.

As we go from smaller to larger atoms by adding one proton at a time to the nucleus and one electron at a time to the electron shells, one other change occurs. As the nucleus grows larger, it acquires neutrons, those uncharged particles that are almost like protons.

The littlest atom, hydrogen, has only one proton in its nucleus and no neutrons. The next atom, number two, is helium. It has two protons in its nucleus, and it also has two neutrons. Thus it has a total of four particles in its nucleus. Two of them are charged, so it acquires two electrons in the outer shells. Next comes lithium, with three protons, three neutrons, and three electrons.

The protons are unable to stick together in combinations unless some neutrons are there also. The protons push each other apart electrically; the only thing that holds them together at all is the short-range forces that work like a layer of glue on the surfaces of the particles. Only when some neutrons are mixed in are the short-range forces strong enough to hold the protons together.

The number of neutrons equals the number of protons in the nucleus of each of the smaller atoms except hydrogen. In the nucleus is just a single proton. As we come to bigger and bigger atoms, though, the nuclei have more neutrons than protons. An iron nucleus has 26 protons and 30 neutrons; iodine has 53 protons and 72 neutrons. The heavier atoms have many more neutrons than protons. The heaviest naturally occurring atom of all, the uranium atom, has 92 protons and 146 neutrons in the nucleus and, of course, 92 electrons on the outside.

At least what I have just said is true if we speak of *most* of the atoms of any element. If you have a bottle filled with hydrogen, almost all of the atoms will have just one proton in the nucleus. But there will be also a small number of very interesting exceptions. Now let us talk of the exceptions.

hydrogen
1 proton

helium
2 protons
2 neutrons

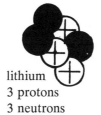

lithium
3 protons
3 neutrons

iron
26 protons
30 neutrons

Big nuclei have more neutrons than protons.

Not all atoms of any one element have just the same number of neutrons in the nucleus. We have spoken of iron with 26 protons and 30 neutrons. It is possible to add or subtract a neutron from the iron nucleus without destroying the atom. Since such an addition or subtraction leaves the same number of protons and the same number of electrons as before, the

33

atom is still an iron atom. In chemical combinations it still behaves like other iron atoms. But it is a little heavier or a little lighter than the other iron atoms around it.

Most iron atoms have 26 protons and 30 neutrons. But there are also iron atoms that have 26, 27, 28, 29, 31, 32, 33, 34, and 35 neutrons. All of them have 26 protons and 26 electrons. All of them combine with atoms of other elements in the same way because the electrons do the mixing and all iron atoms have the same number of electrons, 26. And the reason they all have 26 electrons is that all iron atoms have 26 protons in the nucleus.

The word for a different kind of atom of the same element is "isotope." The element iron has ten different isotopes.

It is not possible to have just any number of neutrons in an iron nucleus. If there are fewer than 26 neutrons or more than 35, the combination comes unstuck. The nucleus in such cases is unstable and will not hold together.

In fact for any element there is a best number of neutrons that makes the nucleus stick together best. As the number of neutrons increases from this number, the sticking gets weaker and weaker until it is not enough to hold a nucleus together at all. Likewise if the number of neutrons becomes gradually smaller than the best number, the sticking becomes weaker and weaker until the nucleus just will not hold together. For example, hydrogen exists in its best, most stable form (the "best model" that we have described) with just one proton in the nucleus. It is best in the sense that almost all hydrogen atoms are made in that way. But a few hydrogen atoms have a proton and one neutron, and a much smaller number have a proton and two neutrons in the nucleus. All are hydrogen because the chemical properties are determined by the one proton and the one electron of all the atoms.

If we could add particles like grapefruits, the entire range of chemical elements that occur in nature could be built up by adding one proton at a time to the nucleus, starting with one and ending at ninety-two. We would arrive at the best-stuck, or most stable, form by adding the best number of neutrons. When we list just the most stable forms we have ninety-two kinds of atoms, one for each chemical element.

The 92 Elements Found in Nature

Atomic Number	Element	Atomic Number	Element
1	hydrogen	27	cobalt
2	helium	28	nickel
3	lithium	29	copper
4	beryllium	30	zinc
5	boron	31	gallium
6	carbon	32	germanium
7	nitrogen	33	arsenic
8	oxygen	34	selenium
9	fluorine	35	bromine
10	neon	36	krypton
11	sodium	37	rubidium
12	magnesium	38	strontium
13	aluminum	39	yttrium
14	silicon	40	zirconium
15	phosphorus	41	niobium
16	sulfur	42	molybdenum
17	chlorine	43	technetium
18	argon	44	ruthenium
19	potassium	45	rhodium
20	calcium	46	palladium
21	scandium	47	silver
22	titanium	48	cadmium
23	vanadium	49	indium
24	chromium	50	tin
25	manganese	51	antimony
26	iron	52	tellurium

Atomic Number	Element	Atomic Number	Element
53	iodine	74	wolfram
54	xenon		(tungsten)
55	cesium	75	rhenium
56	barium	76	osmium
57	lanthanum	77	iridium
58	cerium	78	platinum
59	praseodymium	79	gold
60	neodymium	80	mercury
61	promethium	81	thallium
62	samarium	82	lead
63	europium	83	bismuth
64	gadolinium	84	polonium
65	terbium	85	astatine
66	dysprosium	86	radon
67	holmium	87	francium
68	erbium	88	radium
69	thulium	89	actinium
70	ytterbium	90	thorium
71	lutetium	91	protactinium
72	hafnium	92	uranium
73	tantalum		

Actually we have many more kinds of atoms, because for each chemical element we can have a few more neutrons than the best number or a few less. Counting all the different kinds of atoms that can exist, the total number of kinds of atoms is no longer ninety-two but more than a thousand. On the average, each chemical element exists in more than ten different isotopes with a different number of neutrons in each form. The number of isotopes for any chemical element varies greatly—from only three for hydrogen to more than twenty for some elements.

How many grapefruits and peas would we have to have to

make one model of every kind of atom that nature has put in our great and marvelous universe? It would be a long, patient job to count them all. Yet it would not be impossible. First would come the ninety-two most stable atoms, one for every element, which means one for every number from one to ninety-two. Those ninety-two models would take $1+2+3 \ldots +91+92$ yellow grapefruits. If you can add that series of numbers (and there is a very easy way that you may know already) you will get $93 \times 92/2 = 93 \times 46 = 4,278$ yellow grapefruits.

For each yellow grapefruit in an atom we must have a little green pea to represent an electron; so, 4,278 green peas. In addition, of course we have to have neutrons—not 4,278 neutrons but several more. Only in the smallest atoms are neutron and proton numbers equal. In all the bigger atoms there are more neutrons than protons. So we need more dark grapefruits than yellow ones.

We must have used up more than 15,000 peas and grapefruits already, and so far we have modeled only the ninety-two most stable atoms of the ninety-two elements. We still have to make all the isotopes, and they will bring our numbers to more than eleven times what we have already written. Some of the isotope models will have fewer dark grapefruits than the most stable atom of the same element; some will have more. On the average, though, the ratio of dark to yellow grapefruits will be about the same as for the most stable atoms. So we can multiply whatever our present number really is by eleven and be not too far off. We will need quite a carload of fruit.

· (4) ·

Atoms in a Periodic Table

From the way atoms are constructed comes one of the strange facts about them. Their chemical properties have little or no relation to their nuclear properties.

By chemical properties we mean the way atoms form combinations with other atoms and the way these combinations break up. Wood, for example, is made up mainly of the chemical elements hydrogen, carbon, and oxygen linked together in various kinds of molecules. When wood burns, its hydrogen atoms combine with oxygen (some from the wood and a lot more from the air around it) to form water. Because it is hot, the water forms as steam and blows away. The carbon atoms also combine with oxygen to form carbon dioxide, an invisible gas. On the other hand an electric current passing through water causes the hydrogen and oxygen of which water is made to separate, and they can be made to bubble out, each into its own bottle. Actions in which one atom combines with others or in which a combination breaks up into its parts depend on the electrons around the nucleus.

Nuclear properties, on the other hand, depend only on what happens in the nucleus. In a nuclear reactor, the kind of assembly in which the energy of the nucleus is converted into the heat required to run an electric power plant, free neutrons strike

38

the nuclei of uranium atoms, some of which split into two parts and produce a lot of heat. There are also some atoms that are naturally radioactive. By themselves they give off energetic rays that can make Geiger counters click and can blacken photographic films. These splittings and emissions of radiation occur in the nucleus, and they go on in just the same way whether the atom is all by itself or combined in any way with other atoms.

This separation of chemical and nuclear properties is not surprising when we know the way atoms are made. The distance across the whole atom, including its electrons, is roughly ten thousand times as far as the distance across the tiny nucleus in the middle. So what goes on at the edge of the atom, when it combines with other atoms to form a molecule or separates from them, has little effect on the nucleus that is deep inside. And what happens in the nucleus has little effect on what happens at the edge.

These statements mean that we can usually talk about the nucleus and about the electrons quite separately. A person can study what happens when atoms meet and electron clouds collide and mix with other electron clouds; the subject is chemistry. Then he can look just at the nucleus and what happens when it gains and loses particles, shoots out rays, and breaks in two; the subject is nuclear physics.

About a hundred years ago chemistry took its greatest leap forward. With the single discovery of the periodic table it became vastly simpler—easier to understand. In those days chemists did not know about electrons, protons, neutrons, and the nucleus. So they made their table by using atomic weights, which they did know. But today, if we did not have the table already, we would make it up in a slightly different way (although we would get the same result).

Let us consider how a chemist who needed the table of the elements would make it up by what we now do know about atomic structure. First of all he would remember that all of the chemical elements can be identified by the numbers of electrons in their atoms. Hydrogen has one; helium has two; lithium has three, and so on up to ninety-two if we include only the elements that exist in nature.

A remarkable thing happens if the atoms are put in order by the number of electrons. It turns out that the way they act depends entirely on this number. Some are very active, by which we mean that they are very quick to form links with other atoms and make molecules. Sodium is very active—it causes a burst of flame when a lump of it falls into water. Other elements are very slow to react—like lead, which can lie at the bottom of a pond for years and still come up looking as it did when it went down.

If the elements are put in order according to the numbers of electrons in their atoms and if somebody then goes along the row studying one element after another, he will find, after a few elements, that the properties repeat. For example, an extremely active chemical element will be followed by one not quite so active and then by another still less active. A certain distance farther along will be another very active atom and then one not quite so active and then one still less active. In other ways, too, the behavior of elements will repeat. Because of this repeating pattern, the elements can be arranged in rows and columns so that families of elements that act alike fall together.

The arrangement of the elements according to this repeating pattern is called the periodic table. By "periodic" we refer to something that happens again regularly after a certain time or space. Monday comes periodically once a week, and the period is one week. Telephone poles are spaced periodically along a road, and their period is the distance separating them.

In the days when this periodic table was discovered, scientists did not know that the atoms were in order by number of electrons. But with the discovery of electrons and the construc-

Atoms in a Periodic Table

1	← NUMBER OF ELECTRONS						2
H	← SYMBOL						He
hydrogen	← NAME						helium
3	4	5	6	7	8	9	10
Li	Be	B	C	N	O	F	Ne
lithium	beryllium	boron	carbon	nitrogen	oxygen	fluorine	neon
11	12	13	14	15	16	17	18
Na	Mg	Al	Si	P	S	Cl	Ar
sodium	magnesium	aluminum	silicon	phosphorus	sulfur	chlorine	argon

The first eighteen elements as they fall in the periodic table.

tion of atoms, men could not only make the periodic table, they could also explain it.

The figure on this page shows the first eighteen elements arranged in the periodic table. You will see that reading from left to right along any row is going in the direction of increasing electron number. But what is more remarkable is that reading vertically, one finds elements that behave alike. For example, the column farthest to the right contains helium with two electrons, neon with ten, and argon with eighteen. They are absolutely the most inactive elements of the entire set. All of them are gases without any odor or color. None of them will burn or combine with any other atoms in any way (except for some very rare reactions that chemists have been able to cause in just the last few years).

The arrangement of electrons in these atoms explains why they

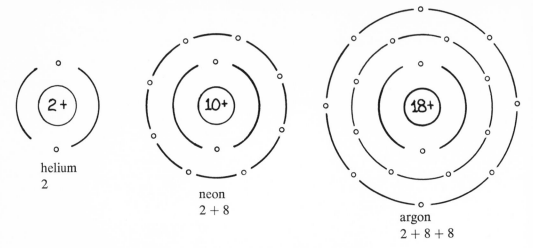

helium
2

neon
2 + 8

argon
2 + 8 + 8

Inert elements have only "closed" (filled) electron shells.

behave as they do. The helium atom has two electrons, and they form a completely filled inner shell—a closed shell, as chemists call it. Because there are no extra electrons looking for something to hold onto and no empty spaces for electrons seeking a place to rest, the atom forms no bonds with other atoms. The next atom in the column, neon, has two closed shells, one with two and one with eight electrons. And argon has three closed shells, two, eight, and eight. So each of these atoms has only electrons in closed shells.

At the opposite side of the table, in the left-hand column, are the most active elements, hydrogen, lithium and sodium (Na). Hydrogen is an odorless gas, but it burns readily in oxygen to produce water. In fact hydrogen is chemically so active that when it is mixed with oxygen, the mixture will explode with a bang. (The explosion is a big one because the two elements are gases, and therefore all the atoms of one can get at all the atoms of the other.) Lithium and sodium are both shiny metals. But they, too, are so active that one seldom sees them shiny. If they are exposed to air, the oxygen that is part of the air immediately combines with them and produces a dull film of oxide on their surfaces. If either of them is dropped into water, the reaction is so violent that a burst of flame immediately appears.

Atoms in a Periodic Table

If one moves horizontally along a row of the periodic table, one finds that the properties of the atoms gradually change. An example would be the way that each element of the middle row combines with atoms of hydrogen. Neon will not combine with hydrogen at all. A fluorine atom combines with one hydrogen atom to make hydrogen fluoride, written HF, which is a liquid at temperatures slightly below room temperature and a gas at higher temperatures. An oxygen atom combines with two atoms of hydrogen to make a water molecule, H_2O. A nitrogen atom combines with three hydrogens to make ammonia, NH_3. A carbon atom combines with four hydrogen atoms to make methane, CH_4. (The atoms in the rest of the row combine differently.)

Just as an atom of hydrogen combines with one atom of fluorine, it combines with one atom of chlorine to make hydrogen chloride. When this dissolves in water, hydrochloric acid is

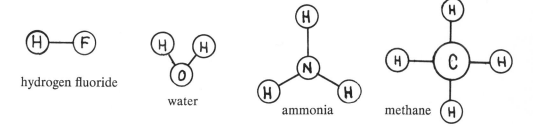

hydrogen fluoride

water

ammonia

methane

Four molecules that show how different atoms combine with different numbers of hydrogen atoms.

formed. So, too, does one atom of sodium (Na) combine with one atom of chlorine to make a molecule of sodium chloride, common table salt, NaCl.

From these facts it can be seen that as one progresses from right to left along a row of the table, atoms combine with more atoms of hydrogen to make common chemical compounds and that atoms in a column (fluorine and chlorine) combine with the same numbers of atoms in another column (hydrogen, lithium, sodium).

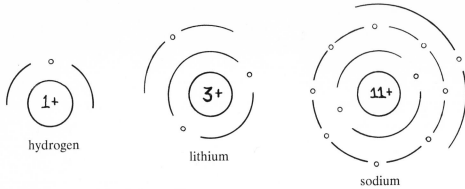

Three atoms that behave alike.

The explanation of all these regularities of behavior and the many other regularities that appear when the full table of ninety-two elements is constructed is in the arrangement of the atoms. In the column at the far left, for instance, are hydrogen, lithium, and sodium. They all behave alike. They are very active and one atom of each of them combines with one atom of fluorine or chlorine. What else do they have in common?

Studying their electrons, we find the answer. Hydrogen has just one electron. Lithium, with three of them, has a closed inner shell of two and a single electron outside. Sodium has a closed inner shell of two, another closed shell of eight, and a single electron outside of that. Each of these atoms, then, has on its very outer edge a single, solitary electron looking for a chance to form a bond with the electrons of another atom.

In the second column from the left are the atoms that have two electrons at the outer edge. Beryllium has a closed inner shell of two electrons and two more outside that closed shell. Magnesium has two closed shells and then two electrons on the outside.

And so it goes across the table until we get to the right-hand column, and there, as we have already said, are the atoms with only closed shells and no electrons outside them. Every atom behaves chemically according to how many electrons are on the outer edge.

We see here also why one hydrogen atom combines with one fluorine atom, but it takes two hydrogen atoms to combine with

44

one oxygen atom. The fluorine atom with seven electrons in its outer shell needs just one more electron to complete that shell. A hydrogen atom, when it combines with the fluorine atom, supplies that missing electron. And the oxygen atom, with six electrons in a shell that has room for eight, needs two hydrogen atoms to supply the two missing electrons. The pattern can be extended, of course, to include each of the atoms in its combinations with each of the others.

Here in the arrangement of the electrons of the atom is the science of chemistry. As it happened in history, the chemical properties, including the weights of the atoms, came first. Chemists made the table. Then physicists discovered the electron, its properties, and the structure of atoms. From the structure they could find out why the table worked.

Of course it could have happened the other way. If electrons and atomic structure had been known first, a periodic table could have been made from the way electrons are arranged in atoms. Then with more exploration scientists could have found out what kinds of chemical reactions to expect among the atoms. They might have built up an explanation of chemical reactions by studying a table of how electrons are arranged in atoms.

Perhaps this second way, making the table from the electron arrangement and then studying its predictions about chemistry, is the easy way to look at matters now that we know enough to do it that way. But no matter how you go about it, the wonder is all there, the wonderful complexity of how the atom goes together and the wonderful simplicity of the whole scheme when it is known well enough to be recognized.

Of course the incomplete table with eighteen elements is only a start. So too are the simple reactions in which one element reacts with one other and only two or three or four atoms take part in a reaction. The complexity increases as the number of elements goes up to ninety-two and the number of atoms goes up to millions in some big molecules. But the start is here and a journey of a thousand miles begins with one small step.

45

·(5)·

Stable and Unstable Nuclei

Just as each atom has a chemical behavior determined by its electrons, it also has a nuclear behavior determined by the particles in its nucleus. To predict the chemical behavior—the way an atom reacts when it meets other atoms or separates from them—we need to know how many electrons are in the outer layers of the atom and how they are arranged. To predict nuclear behavior we need to know how many neutrons and how many protons are in its nucleus. Atoms fall into chemical families that we can represent with a chemist's periodic table, and where they fall depends on the electrons; they fall into nuclear families, too, and nuclear charts tell where.

Take oxygen. Every oxygen atom has eight electrons in two outer shells, two in a closed inner shell and six in a partly filled outer shell. Because the number of electrons in the outer shells must be just equal to the number of protons in the nucleus, the nucleus must have just eight protons. If you could grab one of these oxygen atoms, push one more proton into the nucleus, and then put the atom back where it was, the atom would soon pick up one more electron. But this new atom would no longer be oxygen. It would have become fluorine, which is atom number 9. If a proton and an electron could be taken away from an oxygen atom, it would become nitrogen, atom number 7.

Another change that can occur in the oxygen nucleus, however, will produce a different atom that is still an oxygen atom. This is the addition or subtraction of a neutron. Because the added or subtracted neutron has no charge, the electrons in the outer shells, which are attracted by the charges of the protons in the nucleus, behave after the addition or subtraction just as they did before. They still feel the pull of eight protons and occupy the same places after a neutron is added or taken away as they did before the change.

Most oxygen atoms have sixteen particles in their nuclei— eight protons and eight neutrons. We call them oxygen-16. On close study of many oxygen atoms, however, some of them are found to have one more neutron. In other words, they have nuclei made up of nine neutrons and eight protons, seventeen particles in all, and the label is, therefore, oxygen-17. In fact an oxygen atom can have as few as six neutrons (oxygen-14) and as many as twelve neutrons (oxygen-20) or any number in between.

Because all of these oxygen atoms have eight protons and eight electrons, they all behave chemically the same way. Only the nuclei are different. So there is not one kind of oxygen atom but a family of seven different kinds. The different members of the family are called isotopes. (In Greek "isotope" means "same place," and the interpretation is that all members of this family of isotopes fall in the same place in the chemist's periodic table.) All of them are oxygen even though they are not all exactly alike.

Oxygen is not the only element that has isotopes. In fact, every chemical element has atoms with different numbers of neutrons. In other words, every chemical element has isotopes. The diagram on pages 50–51 shows the isotopes of the first eighteen elements.

A logical question at this point is why atoms do not exist with just any number of neutrons. Why, for example, should helium exist with one, two, three, and four neutrons but not with no neutrons and not with five, six, or seven? The answer has to do with stability.

To see the meaning of this important word, consider three cubical blocks. Suppose, for example, that one block is one foot on each edge—that is, a foot high, a foot wide, and a foot deep. Let the next be half as long on each edge, that is, six inches in each direction—and the third one three inches on each edge.

These three blocks can stand one on top of another in several ways—six, to be exact. The biggest block can be on the bottom, the middle-sized one on top of it, and the smallest one at the top of the pile. In another arrangement the biggest block can be at the bottom, the smallest one next, and the middle-sized one on top. In still another way the smallest one can be at the bottom, the biggest on top, and the middle-sized one in the middle. And so on.

Which pile is least likely to tumble? This is a question of stability. The pile with the greatest stability is least likely to do so. Of the three piles just described, the most stable pile, the one least likely to fall, has the biggest block at the bottom and the smallest one at the top. A bit less stable is the pile with the big block at the bottom and the middle-sized one at the top. And least stable of all is the one that has the smallest block at the bottom.

Other piles of blocks, too, can illustrate this quality of stability. A pile might be made of blocks all of the same size. A pile with just two blocks, one on top of the other, would be very stable, unlikely to fall. A pile of five would be less stable, and one of fifty, all piled in a straight line, one above another, would be terribly unstable. A stable pile of fifty might have twenty-five blocks in a square at the bottom, sixteen blocks in a square on top of them, and so on until the fifty were used up.

48

Stable and Unstable Nuclei

Like piles of blocks, nuclei can be stable or unstable. They can be more or less stable. So if one were to take an oxygen atom with eight protons and eight neutrons (oxygen-16) and add neutrons to it one at a time, the effect would be like adding blocks to a pile. As neutrons were added, one at a time, a number would be reached at which the nucleus would not accept any more. One more neutron would make a nucleus so unstable that it would break up, just as one more block might cause a pile of blocks to tumble.

Even before a pile of blocks actually tumbled, though, it would become shaky. Unstable nuclei are like piles of blocks that will stand only until somebody shakes the floor or opens the door or turns on a fan.

Stability of a nucleus describes how long the nucleus will exist without breaking up and changing into some other kind of nucleus. Some nuclei—most of them, in fact—are entirely stable. They go on forever without changing. Others will change after a very long time, and these are slightly unstable. Still others will change after a very short time; they are very unstable.

Nobody has ever found any way to change the nuclear stability of a particular kind of atom. There is no way to shake the floor, open a door, or turn on a fan and thereby change the rate at which nuclei break up. They break up spontaneously, and nobody can tell when a particular nucleus will break up.

What one can tell about nuclei is that in a very large number of unstable nuclei, all alike, a certain number will break up every second, and half of them will have broken up in a certain amount of time. This time in which half the nuclei will break up is called the "half-life." It is different for each kind of nucleus.

Three of the isotopes of oxygen are stable. In the diagram on pages 50–51 they are represented by the black circles at oxygen-16 (eight neutrons), oxygen-17 (nine) and oxygen-18 (ten).

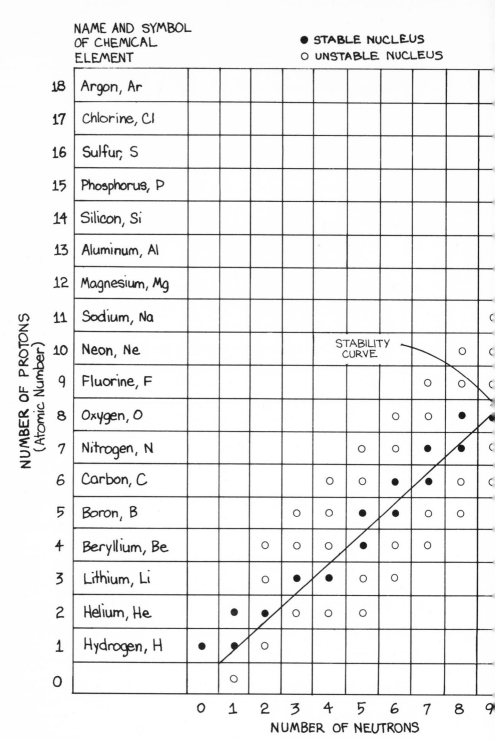

Stable (black circles) and unstable (open circles) isotopes of the first eighteen elements (nineteen if you count the free neutron as "element" number zero). The stability curve passes through the most stable isotope of each element.

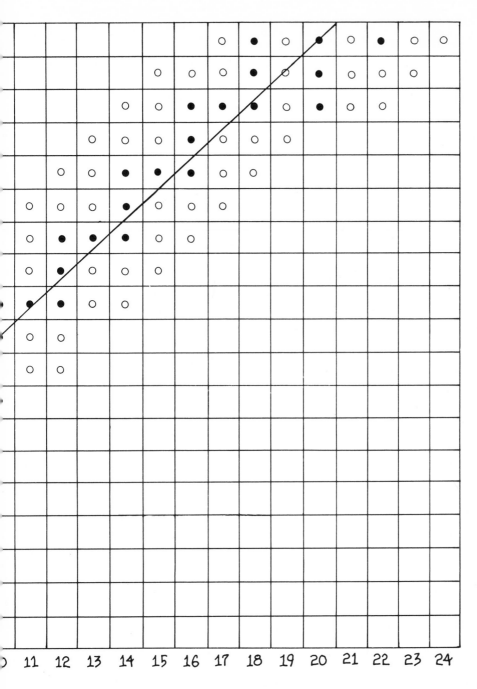

> 11 12 13 14 15 16 17 18 19 20 21 22 23 24

In this diagram each square represents a certain number of protons and a certain number of neutrons in the nucleus. The number of protons can be found by counting up from the bottom: zero for the first row, one for the second, two for the third, and so on to 18. The number of neutrons is

None of the nuclei of these atoms will ever change by itself. Only if a neutron or some other particle hits it from outside will it ever change.

The other four oxygen isotopes, though, are unstable. Oxygen-19 has a half-life of about thirty seconds. This means that if you start with an oxygen-19 sample made up of a million atoms, only half of them will be left unchanged after thirty seconds. After another thirty seconds, half of that half will be left —that is, a quarter of the original sample—and so on. Oxygen-15 has a half-life of about two minutes. The longer half-life means that it is more stable than oxygen-19; it takes about four times as long for half of the atoms of an oxygen-15 sample to break down as for half of the atoms of an oxygen-19 sample to do so. Oxygen-14, with a half-life of about seventy seconds, is more stable than oxygen-19 and less stable than oxygen-15.

The element carbon, which has six electrons and therefore

---

found by counting columns from left to right: zero for the first column at the extreme left, one for the next, two for the next, and so on. The squares that are occupied by a round dot or circle represent those nuclei that exist. For example, the simple hydrogen atom, which has just one proton in the nucleus and no neutrons, has a black dot at the position for one proton and no neutrons. Beside it to the right is the hydrogen atom with one proton and one neutron. It is called deuterium. Next to the right is tritium, the hydrogen atom with one proton and two neutrons in its nucleus. The next square to the right is empty, and this fact means that no hydrogen atom has one proton and three neutrons.

The three dots in the hydrogen row of the figure represent the three isotopes of hydrogen.

One row above are the isotopes of helium. They start with helium-3 with two protons and one neutron, and they go on through helium-4 and helium-5 and helium-6 to helium-7, which has two protons and five neutrons. In this way the various rows show the different isotopes of the first 18 elements. The row corresponding to eight protons shows the oxygen isotopes. A count of the dots shows that the first 18 elements have a total of 119 isotopes. (This does not count the dot for one neutron, no proton, because the neutron alone does not form an atom.)

falls just two steps before oxygen in the periodic table, has a more typical set of isotopes than oxygen. The isotopes, with their half-lives, are as follows:

C-10	19 seconds
C-11	20 minutes
C-12	stable
C-13	stable
C-14	5700 years
C-15	2 seconds
C-16	0.74 second

The word "stable" means that the isotopes carbon-12 and carbon-13 do not break up at all by themselves; unless disturbed by something from outside, they last forever. So one way to describe a stable isotope is to say it has a half-life of infinity. This word stands for a time so very, very long that it might as well be forever. If the word "stable" is replaced with the word "infinity," the list of the carbon isotopes shows an interesting pattern. As one goes through the list from the lightest isotopes to the heaviest ones, the half-lives start very short, increase to infinity, and then decrease again to very short.

This characteristic is typical of most of the isotopes in the entire table, and it leads to a regularity that one can see in the table on pages 50–51. Of the isotopes represented there, the stable ones (solid black dots) usually lie in the center of the band of all isotopes. This feature is equivalent to the following statements: For any element there is a pair of numbers of protons and neutrons that makes the most stable combination. This most stable combination is usually near the middle of the list of isotopes of that element. Isotopes that have more neutrons or fewer neutrons than the most stable number are gradually less stable the farther away their number is from the most stable combination. (Sometimes an exception occurs and two stable isotopes have an unstable one between them. The explanation is that stability depends on the proton number as well as the neutron number. So we have to look up and down in the diagram as well as left and right to see whether any atom is more stable than its neighbors.)

The chart of all isotopes of all elements (including man-made elements) has about 1600 different entries at the present time. (More can be discovered any day.) Through this entire chart, which is an extension of the chart of the first eighteen elements on page 41, a stability curve can be drawn. This is a line that goes through the most stable combination for each element in the table, and it shows the number of neutrons that makes the most stable nucleus for each element. In general, the closer any nucleus is to this line, the more stable it is; the farther away, the less stable.

A study of all the 1600 isotopes in a complete diagram shows other interesting patterns in the stability of isotopes. Some of them can be seen even in the diagram of the first eighteen elements on page 41. For example, some elements have more stable isotopes than others. Hydrogen, helium, and lithium have two each, but beryllium, which comes next, has only one. Neon, element number 10, has three. Although most elements have all their stable isotopes in the center near the stability curve, some, like chlorine, have unstable ones in the center with stable ones on both sides.

As one looks along the table of all elements to those of bigger and bigger atomic number, one finds proportionately more unstable isotopes than stable ones. Finally, when one gets to lead, which is element number 82, one has passed all of the stable isotopes. All isotopes of all elements with atomic numbers greater than 82 are unstable.

Most of the atoms that make up our universe are stable. On the chart on pages 50–51 they occupy the positions of solid black dots. For example, more than ninety-nine per cent of all oxygen

54

atoms are atoms of oxygen-16, the most stable isotope. The remaining atoms, much less than one per cent of all oxygen atoms, are distributed among the other six oxygen isotopes.

These stable isotopes will never change unless something hits them from outside and causes the change. Whatever hits and causes a change must not hit only the atom; it must hit the tiny nucleus itself. Direct hits are very rare. The nucleus is surrounded by an outer cloud of electrons. If anything breaks through the outer cloud, it faces the charge of the nucleus. This charge will push away any other positively charged particle with a force that becomes enormous when the invading body gets near enough to threaten damage. Only a neutron can approach the nucleus without being pushed away by either the electrons or the nuclear charge, and there are very few unattached neutrons around.

The unstable nuclei represented by circles in the diagram are quite different from the stable ones. They are like unstable piles of blocks that will not stand but will tumble because of their instability. Unlike an unstable pile of blocks, though, they do not need a shake of the floor to make them tumble. Of their own accord, with no influence from outside, they will change into more stable nuclei.

An unstable nucleus is like an unstable pile of blocks ready to tumble to the floor. But having no floor to tumble to, it finds its own way to greater stability. It shoots out a bit of radiation and becomes a different kind of nucleus. It may perform this act several times, but eventually it changes itself into one of the stable nuclei and then just remains that way. The pile of blocks has fallen all the way.

The radiation that comes away from these changing nuclei is very powerful. Sometimes it is charged particles coming away at great speed; sometimes it is powerful electrical vibrations like the x rays that come from a doctor's machine.

The name for the processes by which unstable nuclei change

to more stable ones is radioactivity. The atoms that undergo change are called radioactive atoms; the materials that they make up are called radioactive materials, and the rays that they give off are called radioactive emissions.

Of course there are millions and millions of ways in which you could stick honey-covered yellow and dark grapefruits together. When protons and neutrons are stuck together by nature, though, the laws of nature determine that only about 1600 of these patterns correspond to nuclei. By laws of nature we really mean the forces that act among the nuclear particles —the electric force among protons and the nuclear force among both protons and neutrons.

And out of these 1600 patterns that make nuclei, a small number correspond to the truly stable nuclei that never change by themselves. Of the nuclei in our world, however, only a few correspond to the unstable patterns. Most of the nuclei in ourselves and the materials around us are quite stable, unlikely ever to change. Otherwise this rapidly changing world of ours would be changing much more rapidly than it is already.

·(6)·

Radioactivity

A chart that shows all the kinds of nuclei (a full version of the one on pages 50–51) has many more places for unstable nuclei than for stable ones. Nevertheless most of the atoms of the universe have stable nuclei because many more actual nuclei correspond to the stable patterns than to the unstable ones.

A dress manufacturer might have as many patterns for evening dresses as for housedresses. But if he tells the people who cut and sew to make a hundred copies of each housedress pattern and only two copies of each evening dress pattern, the racks will have fifty times as many housedresses as evening dresses. Nuclei are in a similar situation; there are more patterns for unstable nuclei but many more copies of each stable pattern.

This situation tells us why most of the atoms we come into contact with every day—those in water, wood, and food—are not radioactive. Yet radioactive atoms, though few by comparison, are very interesting to us because of the unusual things they do.

Almost any unstable system—a rolling wheel, a boy on stilts, a pile of blocks, or an unstable nucleus—tends to change to a more stable arrangement when it has the chance. The wheel and the boy fall to the ground; some of the blocks tumble to the floor; the nucleus changes to a different nucleus.

57

The unstable nucleus has its own particular way of finding a more stable arrangement. In general, no matter where the nucleus is in the chart of the isotopes it will change into another nucleus that is nearer to the stability curve. Several distinct steps are involved in the change from one to the other.

The first essential step is the birth of a particle in the nucleus. Of course the nucleus already has particles—the neutrons and protons. Yet for purposes of radioactivity a new and different particle must be born from the stuff that makes up neutrons and protons.

Step two in the process is the throwing out, or emission, of the newly created particle. It is emitted with tremendous energy, in other words with great speed. You can think of the forces that bind particles in the nucleus and those that hold electrons on the outside as if they were stretched rubber bands. If the band is a small one (like the forces that hold electrons) nothing much happens when you break it. But the forces in the nucleus are typically a million times as strong as those that hold electrons. When a particle is emitted from the nucleus, the action is like breaking not just a stretched elastic band but a stretched automobile tire or a stretched conveyer belt. The commotion is enormous. In breaking such great forces the emitted particle gets its enormous speed, and it crashes with a strong impact into whatever it strikes after it gets out of the nucleus, scattering electrons in all directions.

The last step in the change is often the emission of electromagnetic rays, which are called gamma rays. They do not have mass or charge, like the particle that starts the process. Still, they have a lot of energy, and they, too, can cause quite a commotion. They are like light waves, but they are much more powerful.

What causes the electromagnetic rays to come away is that the new nucleus that is made when a particle is emitted has not yet found its most stable arrangement. A block has been

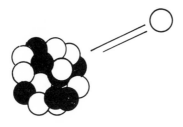

Radioactive emission. A particle is expelled at great speed.

pushed out of the pile, but the other blocks, without leaving the pile, rearrange themselves and lose energy as they do so. That energy comes out as gamma rays.

Perhaps it is appropriate to say that this act of disintegration in a nucleus is like the firing of a cannon in a canyon. Out comes the particle like a cannonball, with tremendous speed and energy. Then, a little later, come the reverberations. The firing of the cannon dislodges rocks from the canyon walls, and as they fall, some of their energy comes booming out of the canyon as sound waves. In the nucleus the particle emitted is the cannonball, and as other particles in the nucleus shake down into more comfortable positions, the gamma rays come out like reverberations that are echoes of the boom and the noise of rocks dislodged by the firing.

After the disintegration has occurred, the new nucleus must be more stable than the one before it, but it need not be altogether stable. The new nucleus may be radioactive also. Like the original nucleus, it may go through a disintegration. Then the next nucleus may be radioactive, and so on. Eventually the chain of disintegrations stops when a stable pattern is reached, but it is not uncommon for the chain to have ten or twelve steps before it ends with a stable nucleus.

The three principal kinds of radiation that come from nuclei were labeled with the first three letters of the Greek alphabet when scientists could observe them but did not yet understand

59

them. Alpha and beta rays are the emitted particles with charge and mass. The electromagnetic rays are called gamma rays.

An alpha particle is a very tightly bound combination of two neutrons and two protons. They have to come together in the nucleus, form the tightly bound combination, and then be ejected from the nucleus before an alpha ray can come into existence. Most nuclei of the heaviest atoms decay by emitting alpha particles.

If you look at a chart of all the nuclei, you will see that the nucleus of the common helium atom, helium-4, also has two neutrons and two protons just as the alpha particle does. In fact the helium nucleus is identical with the alpha particle, and helium is formed wherever alpha emission takes place. One bit of evidence that showed scientists what alpha particles are was this formation of helium around substances emitting alpha radiation.

Beta particles come in two kinds, positive and negative. The negative ones are just like the electrons that make up the outer layers of atoms. In fact after it has been emitted and after it has bounced around long enough to slow down, a negative beta particle becomes a simple electron and takes its place in the outer shell of another atom.

A nucleus is made up of only protons and neutrons. Yet it can emit a negative beta particle, which is (except for its great speed) just like an ordinary electron. The explanation is that the nucleus makes the beta particle as it emits it.

Positive beta particles are just like the negative ones except that their charge is positive instead of negative. They, too, are made in the nucleus when they are emitted. In this case, though, a proton changes into a neutron plus a positive beta particle; the beta particle is immediately expelled with great speed.

The world is a very unfriendly place for positive beta particles, or, as they are usually called, positrons. Whenever a positron is emitted, it finds itself in a great sea of negative electrons

alpha particle   negative beta particle   positive beta particle (positron)

Three kinds of radioactive emissions—alpha, negative beta, positive beta.

—all the electrons that make up all the outer layers of all the atoms around it. A positron is attracted to these electrons that have the opposite kind of electric charge, and eventually it bumps into one. When it does, there is a great flash of light (we could almost say, an explosion), and both positron and electron disappear. In fact nothing is left but the radiation emitted in the explosion. Scientists say that the two particles have annihilated each other. In Latin *nihil* is the word for "nothing," so the meaning is that the two particles have "made each other into nothing."

The gamma rays are part of what we call the electromagnetic spectrum, that is, all of the different kinds of electromagnetic waves that are parts of everyday life. The ones with longest wavelength are the radio waves like those that carry radio and television signals. Shorter waves are the heat waves like the ones from glowing coals and steam radiators. Shorter still are visible light waves with which we see things. Next come the ultraviolet rays that cause sunburn and x rays that doctors can use to see broken bones. Shortest of all are the gamma rays. Because as wavelengths become shorter, waves become more powerful and more penetrating, gamma rays are the most powerful of all.

Although alpha, beta, and gamma disintegrations are the ways by which most unstable nuclei find arrangements of greater stability, some nuclei find other ways. Some have a choice between two or more ways of decaying—for example, either by alpha-particle emission or by beta-particle emission—just as an unstable pile of blocks might tumble either to the left or to the right. Some nuclei become more stable by grabbing one of the

61

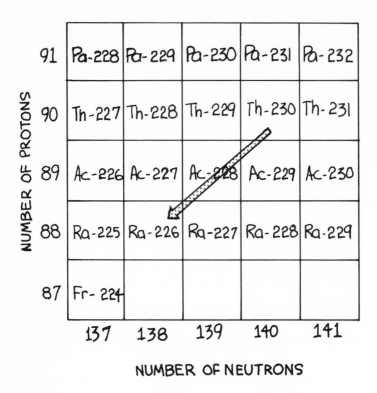

The chart shows a grid with "NUMBER OF PROTONS" on the vertical axis and "NUMBER OF NEUTRONS" on the horizontal axis.

	137	138	139	140	141
91	Pa-228	Pa-229	Pa-230	Pa-231	Pa-232
90	Th-227	Th-228	Th-229	Th-230	Th-231
89	Ac-226	Ac-227	Ac-228	Ac-229	Ac-230
88	Ra-225	Ra-226	Ra-227	Ra-228	Ra-229
87	Fr-224				

NUMBER OF NEUTRONS

Thorium-230 emits an alpha particle to become radium-226.

electrons from the outer layers of the atom and adding the electron to a proton, making a proton into a neutron. But most radioactive disintegrations are simply emissions of alpha, beta, and gamma rays.

After the radiation has left the nucleus, what can we say about the nucleus? How has it changed? What new position has it taken in the chart that shows all nuclei?

If the radiation is an alpha particle, the original nucleus has lost two protons and two neutrons. To find the new nucleus in the chart, we must start from the original position and move two spaces to the left (two protons fewer) and two spaces down (two neutrons fewer). On this page is a section of the chart we have when we extend the figure on pages 50–51 to include all isotopes of all elements. An arrow shows how thorium-230 becomes radium-226 with emission of an alpha particle. The same kind of change occurs when any other nucleus emits an alpha particle.

When a beta particle is emitted, either a neutron changes into a proton or a proton changes into a neutron. If the beta particle is negative, a neutron has changed into a proton; if it is positive, a proton has become a neutron. Notice that charge is conserved, by which we mean that if we could put all the charges back together, we would have the same amount that we started with. When a neutron becomes a proton plus a negative beta particle, we have one negative charge and one positive charge. Put together they would cancel each other; in other words, minus one and plus one add up to the zero we had at first. Likewise, when a proton becomes a positron plus a neutron, we start with one positive charge and end with one positive charge.

The new nucleus, if the beta particle is negative, has one more proton and one less neutron. The section of chart on page 64 shows the change that occurs when oxygen-19 emits a negative beta particle to become fluorine-19. The one on page 65 shows how, with positron emission, oxygen-15 becomes nitrogen-15. You can see that in both situations unstable nuclei have moved toward the stability curve and become stable nuclei.

A peculiarity of a radioactive atom is that nobody can tell just when it will disintegrate. It is just as likely to disintegrate in the very next second as in the first second of the next day or the first second of the next year. But when a lot of these atoms —say a million or a million million—are together in one place it is possible to say that, on the average, a certain number of them will disintegrate in the next second.

On a lonely country road where few persons walk you might have to wait half a day or half a year for a man to come along with a black hat on his head. But when you watch people coming away from a big football game, you can expect to see a certain number of men coming by in each minute, and a certain number of them are likely to be wearing black hats.

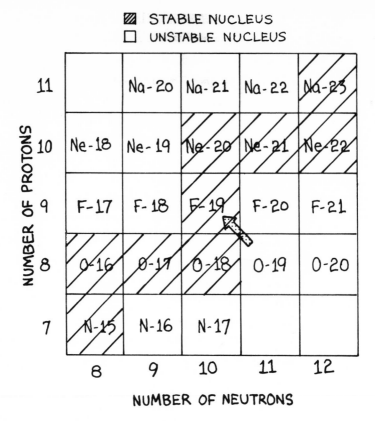

11		Na-20	Na-21	Na-22	Na-23
10	Ne-18	Ne-19	Ne-20	Ne-21	Ne-22
9	F-17	F-18	F-19	F-20	F-21
8	O-16	O-17	O-18	O-19	O-20
7	N-15	N-16	N-17		
	8	**9**	**10**	**11**	**12**

NUMBER OF PROTONS (vertical axis)

NUMBER OF NEUTRONS

Oxygen-19 emits a negative electron; a neutron becomes a proton; the atom becomes fluorine-19.

The behavior of a large number of atoms is similar. Just as you cannot tell when you first see him in the distance whether the next man will have a black hat, you cannot tell in advance when any particular atom will disintegrate. But if you have many of them, you can tell that a certain portion will go off in a certain time.

To indicate how fast any particular kind of nucleus disintegrates, scientists tell its half-life—the time required for half of the atoms in a large number to disintegrate. If the half-life is one day and the sample has a million atoms, then about half of them will have disintegrated in a day; half of the ones that are left will disintegrate in the next day; half of the ones left then will disintegrate in the next day, and so on.

The radiations from radioactive nuclei are useful in two ways.

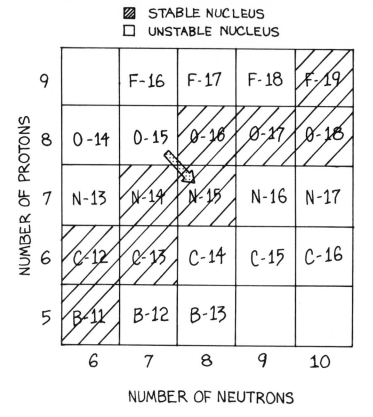

Oxygen-15 emits a positron; a proton becomes a neutron; the atom becomes nitrogen-15.

First, the radiations always indicate where the radioactive atoms are. As radioactive atoms flow down a sink pipe and down a river, as they go through various chemical reactions, they continue to give off their radiations. With instruments that click when radiation hits them and with other means of detection such as photographic film, a scientist can follow these atoms. He can see which ones go into a chemical reaction, which ones go into the bloodstream of a person taking medicine, and into which parts of a plant the nourishment flows from the soil.

The other way in which radiation from radioactivity is useful—and sometimes inconvenient—is that the radiation itself can cause things to happen to matter exposed to it. The radiations are powerful. When they strike other atoms they knock

65

electrons out of their usual places, they break up chemical molecules, and they cause new chemical reactions. Some of these reactions are useful. The plastic coating of an insulated wire can be made tough by exposure to radiations. And some actions are harmful. A person can be burned by overexposure to radiation.

Radioactivity and the different kinds of radiation it produces have been fascinating subjects for scientists ever since they were discovered at the beginning of this century. By observing the radiations, physicists have found out which nuclei are stable, which are unstable, and how the unstable ones change to become more stable. Using radiation as an indicator of where radioactive atoms are, chemists and biologists have found out much about chemical and biological processes. And the way that these radiations affect living and non-living materials has shown a great deal about the materials and the ways that atoms are bound together to make them.

·(7)·

Effects of Radiation

When radioactive atoms disintegrate, they emit alpha, beta, and gamma rays. In a group of them big enough for scientists to work with, there might be millions of millions of atoms, and thousands of millions of them might be disintegrating in each second. The radiation might be coming from just one kind of atom and be all alpha or all beta or all gamma radiation. It might also come from a mixture of atoms, and the source might be emitting all three kinds of radiation at once.

Whether the radiation is alpha, beta, gamma, or a mixture, each burst of it comes away from the nucleus with tremendous energy. In view of the minuteness of the particles on which they act, nuclear forces are enormous. When a burst of radiation comes out of the nucleus, the forces that are broken are millions of times greater than the forces binding electrons to the outer shells of the atom.

Because great forces are broken and the emitted radiation comes away with tremendous energy and speed, it has some mighty effects on the matter that is around it. Somewhere in its travel, each burst of radiation must strike some atoms. It may go a long way before it strikes anything if the source is surrounded by a gas, because there are vast empty spaces between atoms. It may go a much shorter distance if it is surrounded by a liquid or a solid. But somewhere it strikes some atoms, and when it does it raises a great commotion among them. It scatters electrons left and right, thousands of them. Where these electrons have formed chemical bonds, the action breaks up chemical molecules. Then, because many electrons that have been scattered are wandering around free, new molecules can form. As a result of the radiation, all these changes cause great and noticeable effects.

To see just what happens and why it happens, one can think about an alpha particle emitted from an atom and plunging through other atoms around the source. Surrounding the emitted particle is a vast sea of electrons—all the electrons that form the outer shells of all the atoms in the neighborhood.

Of course there are atomic nuclei too, but they are not very important to the emitted alpha particle. Two reasons explain this lack of importance. The first is that the nuclei are so very, very small. The nucleus is only a ten thousandth as wide as the whole atom, whereas the electron or electrons spread out to fill the whole atom. So the alpha particle encounters many times as many electrons as it does nuclei.

The second reason is that the nuclei are many thousands of times heavier than the electrons. In a hydrogen atom, which has the lightest nucleus, the nucleus is almost two thousand times as heavy as the electron. All other nuclei are bigger still. As a result, not much happens when an alpha particle hits a nucleus. Although a strong force acts between them, the nucleus is so heavy that the alpha particle has little effect on it. It just bounces off and keeps on going. The collision is a bit like a golf ball hitting a bowling ball. The little golf ball bounces off the bowling ball without noticeably moving the bowling ball and without losing much of its speed.

Quite different things happen, though, when a speeding alpha particle passes near an electron. A strong force acts between them. The alpha particle carries two positive charges; the elec-

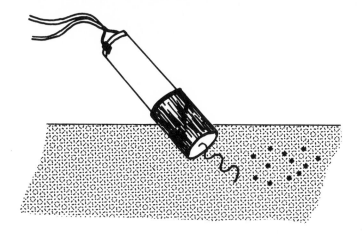

Following radioactive atoms with a Geiger counter that clicks as they pass.

tron has a single negative charge. So they are strongly attracted. The electron is relatively light, and the alpha particle is heavy —about seven thousand times as heavy as the electron. The situation, therefore, is like throwing a golf ball at great speed into a bunch of ping-pong balls. The heavy alpha particle goes speeding along its path in a straight line and is not deflected by the tiny electrons it passes. But the tiny electrons, attracted by a mighty force as the alpha particle goes by, are torn from their atoms and scattered all about.

A huge number of electrons is torn loose and scattered before the alpha particle transfers all of its energy, slows down, and

A speeding alpha particle scatters electrons.

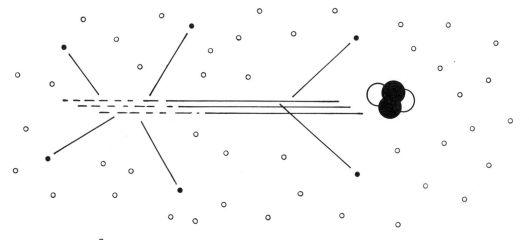

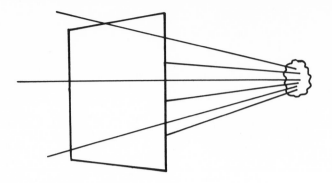

A sheet of paper stops alpha particles.

finally stops. Typically, an alpha particle will scatter a hundred thousand electrons in the course of its flight.

The number is large, and yet all of this scattering occurs in a very small distance. Atoms are so small, and electrons so densely packed, that an alpha particle encounters the electrons required to stop it before it has gone a distance equal to the thickness of a sheet of paper. A sheet of paper held over a source of alpha particles will stop all of them from getting through.

Like the alpha particle, a beta particle comes speeding out of the nucleus carrying electric charge. It too encounters the sea of electrons surrounding all the atoms nearby and scatters them. Unlike the alpha particle, though, a beta particle is not heavier than the electrons it encounters; in fact it is just like them. Instead of a golf ball thrown into a bunch of ping-pong balls, it is more like a ping-pong ball thrown at a lot of other ping-pong balls.

When the speeding beta particle meets an electron, the electric forces between the two pull them together or push them apart. (Whether the force is a push or a pull depends on whether the beta particle is a positive or a negative one.) But because the two particles are alike, not only is the still electron bounced out of its place, but also the beta particle may be deflected from its path. Because the incoming beta particle can

70

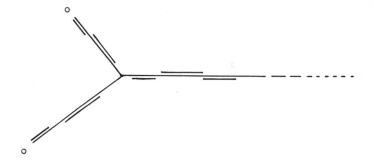

Beta particles bounce off electrons.

bounce away when it makes a collision, it loses less energy than would a heavy alpha particle that came along the same path. Often it collides without dislodging the electrons it hits. So the beta particle has to make a lot more collisions than an alpha particle before it stops. Before it makes all of these collisions, it can wander quite a distance among the electrons that are stopping it and the atoms of which they are parts. In other words, beta particles penetrate farther into matter than alpha particles do before each one dislodges the electrons (about a hundred thousand) required to stop it. It takes more than a sheet of paper to stop all the beta particles from a radioactive source. It takes a sheet of tin or iron or some other material equally massive.

Gamma rays are quite different from both alpha and beta particles, being little bundles of electromagnetic energy like light and x rays. Yet they, too, are stopped by electrons of atoms. The collisions they have are not caused by forces between charges, because gamma rays have no charge. Instead, the gamma ray enters the material as a powerful electric vibration. It produces a vibrating force and shakes an occasional electron out of its atom as the sound wave from a cannon might dislodge a rock from a nearby cliff. Sometimes the gamma ray bounces away from an electron, which gets dislodged from its atom, and then the gamma ray hits another electron and dislodges that one

71

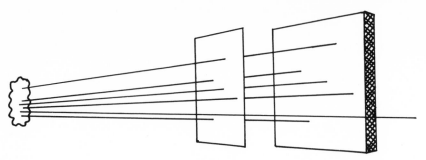

Beta rays pass through paper but stop in lead or tin or iron.

also. The net result, after many collisions, is that the gamma ray has given all its energy to the electrons, and it disappears. Some electrons have been torn away from their atoms.

Gamma rays penetrate into material even farther than beta rays and much farther than alpha particles because their encounters with electrons are by chance; they do not push or pull on every electron near their path as do alpha and beta particles. Thus neither paper nor a thin sheet of metal can be counted on to stop all the gammas from a gamma source. It takes something like a thick piece of metal, a concrete wall or a thick shield full of water.

The actions by which radiations from radioactive atoms affect the atoms near them also permit detection of the radiations. One of the oldest methods for detection is the one that lets you see a television picture. When a bright spot appears on a TV screen, it indicates that some electrons, after traveling down the tube under the influence of electric and magnetic forces, have struck the screen at that point. When they strike, they knock some electrons out of the atoms they belong to. Then, as the

Gamma rays bounce off electrons.

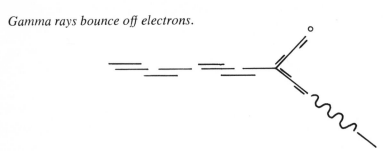

electrons return to atoms that have room for them, they give off light.

If the same TV screen is held near a radioactive source so that alpha, beta, or gamma rays can strike it, it emits light in the same manner. A scientist can count the flashes to see how much radioactivity is present.

Another way to detect radiation is with a Geiger counter, a device that responds to electrons knocked out of atoms. It is a cylindrical glass or metal tube with a fine wire down its center. Air is pumped out, and a special mixture, at low pressure, is put into the tube. A large electric voltage is connected between the wall of the tube and the wire at the center. Then if radiation enters the tube and knocks electrons out of some atoms of the gas, a spark jumps between the wire and the walls of the tube. The tube can be attached to a loudspeaker that will make a loud click every time a bit of radiation causes a spark to jump, and it can be connected to a counter that will tell how many times sparks have jumped.

Since the invention of the transistor and similar devices, tiny crystal-like bits of material connected into electrical circuits have been used to do the job of Geiger counters. They are smaller, cheaper, and easier to use.

Radiation that strikes photographic film will register on it just as light does when it comes through a camera lens. Photographic film is laid against a source of radioactivity, and when it is developed, it shows where the radioactivity was. The method can be used, for example, to show where radioactive materials are present in the leaf of a growing tree. The leaf is laid against the film and left for a while. When the film is developed, dark areas show where there was radioactivity.

Significant changes often occur in matter that is exposed to radiations from radioactive atoms. The fact is not surprising when one thinks what a severe sunburn a person can get by falling asleep and lying too long on the beach. The rays of the

73

sun are like those of radioactivity. In fact the radiations from radioactive nuclei are much more penetrating than the sun's rays. They are often called "ionizing radiation" to show how powerful they are. The adjective "ionizing" refers to the ability these radiations have to knock electrons out of atoms and form ions. (The word "ion" means an atom that has lost or gained electrons.)

Now one or two or even a few hundred alpha, beta, or gamma rays would not cause significant effects. Such amounts of radiation come from outer space and go through our bodies each second, and we do not notice them. But the effects become important when large quantities of radiation are involved.

Most of the materials in everyday life—water, wood, flesh, and the like—are made of molecules, and the molecules are made of atoms tied together by electrons. When a source of radiation is brought near any of these materials, many of the electrons that form chemical bonds are knocked out of place. Bonds are broken; atoms are released; both atoms and electrons wander around forming new combinations. Often these combinations are new kinds that would not have formed if the radiation had not been there to start the reaction.

An interesting example is the cross-linking of polymers. Polymers are long chainlike molecules that form most common

Ionizing radiation dislodges electrons from atoms.

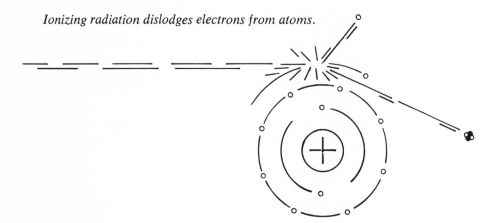

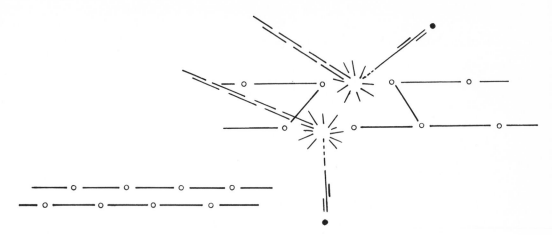

Polymers—long chain molecules—can be cross-linked by radiation.

plastics. Often when these plastics are first formed they are soft. They are composed of chains that lie alongside each other, not tied together. Ionizing radiation affects some of these polymers by breaking free some of the bonding electrons, which then fall into new positions tying together the side-by-side chains. This action makes the plastic tougher, and it softens only at a higher temperature than before the exposure to radiation.

Living things can be killed by exposure to too much radiation. For example bacteria, which die when objects are sterilized by boiling, also die if they are irradiated enough. Radiation sterilization has found useful commercial applications with items that are damaged if they are sterilized with heat. One example is surgical sutures, those strips of animal intestines and other materials with which doctors sew up cuts and wounds. Radiation is used to sterilize many of these sutures when they are prepared.

Cancer often occurs as a tumor, a lump of unwanted tissue that grows very rapidly. Some cancerous tumors are very sensitive to ionizing radiation. Large amounts of radiation damage all tissues, those that are good as well as those that are bad, but the object is to kill the bad tissue of a cancerous tumor more rapidly than the tissue around it.

Accidental exposure to any source of ionizing radiation can

75

cause serious damage to any animal or plant. Thus when large amounts of radioactive material are present anywhere—in a machine used by a hospital to treat cancer or in a nuclear reactor that produces electric power—protective shielding made of lead, steel, concrete, or other dense materials is used. The shielding stops the rays so that accidental exposures do not occur.

Imagine a big room—a gymnasium or a ballroom—with millions of ping-pong balls suspended on tiny threads. Now let a golfer, swinging with all his might, drive a golf ball into that room. The effect will be like that of radiation, where an alpha particle scatters electrons. What a lot of scattering and bouncing will go on!

Then if a mighty David can use his sling with all his skill, he might hurl a ping-pong ball among the others. The effect would be like that of a beta particle bouncing around, scattering the electrons as it comes to them.

And finally we think of a mighty electromagnetic oscillation, a gamma ray, scattering electrons as the boom of a great cannon might scatter our ping-pong balls.

Here we have the effects of radiation from radioactive atoms —fast, powerful, destructive—sometimes useful and sometimes harmful, but always interesting.

· (8) ·

Detective Work
with Radioactivity

At times an airplane cannot be seen in the sky because it is too far away or because its color blends into the sky. Yet its track may be plainly visible, either because it is leaving a trail of black smoke or because its passage through cool, moist air is making a white trail of condensed water vapor.

In many useful applications of radioactivity, the radiations from nuclei are used like the black smoke or the white condensation trail. These nuclei, of course, are parts of atoms, and no matter where these atoms go, their nuclei keep sending out powerful rays. All the scientist who wants to follow them has to do is turn on his Geiger counter or expose a photographic film, and the results will tell him just where the atoms are.

One characteristic that makes radiations especially useful for following atoms is their constancy. In a quantity of radioactive atoms a certain number will disintegrate every second no matter what happens to them. Neither heat nor cold, neither chemical reaction nor physical stress will change the disintegration rate.

Another property that increases the usefulness is that the radiation comes only from the radioactive nucleus and not from the outer layers of the atom. The electrons of the atoms outside the

nucleus are not affected by the radioactivity. Thus the radioactive atom behaves just like the non-radioactive, stable isotopes
of the same element until it disintegrates and fires out its telltale
radiation. If a chemist wants to determine how any chemical element behaves, he can use the radioactive isotopes of the element
in a reaction. The radiation tells him where the atoms go.

Wherever they go these atoms give out powerful alpha, beta,
or gamma rays, and the scientist following them can turn on his
Geiger counter to find out just where they are. In some situations he may use other means of detection such as photographic
film, but by one means or another detection is usually fairly
easy.

The man who wants to use radioactivity to follow something
first has to label it. This means that he puts the radioactive
material where it will serve his purposes. A chemist might have
a problem in which he wants to follow the atoms of a chemical
element like sulfur. He might have a process for combining sulfur with oxygen, and he might want to know how much sulfur
combines with oxygen and how much is left over in the waste.
Then he mixes some radioactive sulfur atoms with the stable
sulfur he is using so that he has labeled sulfur. After making the
sulfur dioxide, he can expose it to his detector to see how much
of the radioactivity has gotten into the sulfur dioxide.

Labeling is more complicated if he wants to follow a chemical
molecule. For instance, a pollution fighter wants to know how
much of the sulfur dioxide coming out of a chimney fails to blow
away with the wind and stays in the city. He can get some radioactive sulfur. A chemist makes it into sulfur dioxide by making
it react with oxygen. Then the experimenter can put the labeled—radioactive—sulfur dioxide into his chimney with the
smoke. With a Geiger counter he can go to the street to determine whether sulfur dioxide from the chimney is settling to the
ground or blowing away. The number of clicks from his counter

will indicate how much of the sulfur dioxide has reached the street.

Which of several ways a scientist will use to mix his radioactive isotope with the material he wants to follow depends on his problem. After he has decided on the isotope he will use for a tracer and the method to label what he wants to trace, he must choose the appropriate means for detection.

Which detector to use also depends on the problem. For example, if radioactive fertilizer is fed to the root system of a plant and the problem is to see which parts of a leaf receive the food, photographic film will get a picture of the distribution.

A technician in the radioactive scanning department of a large city hospital regulates a computer that will produce x rays showing the amount and location of radioactive iodine in the thyroid gland.

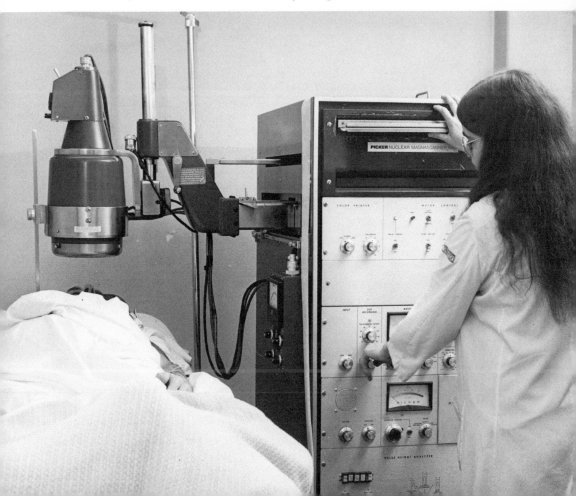

A golf ball could not hide in tall grass if it had a bit of radioactive material at the center emitting gamma rays. The caddy looking for a golf ball would carry a clicking Geiger counter. A chemist studying a liquid might run it through a counting tube, or he might dip a special counting tube into the liquid. Many, many different ways to use radioactive isotopes as tracers have been devised, and new ones are found every day.

An airplane manufacturer once had difficulty because small tools were likely to be lost in a plane while it was being built. The plane was large; the tools were small, and it was hard to

A doctor studies the outlines of a thyroid tumor revealed in x rays taken by the radioactive scanning device.

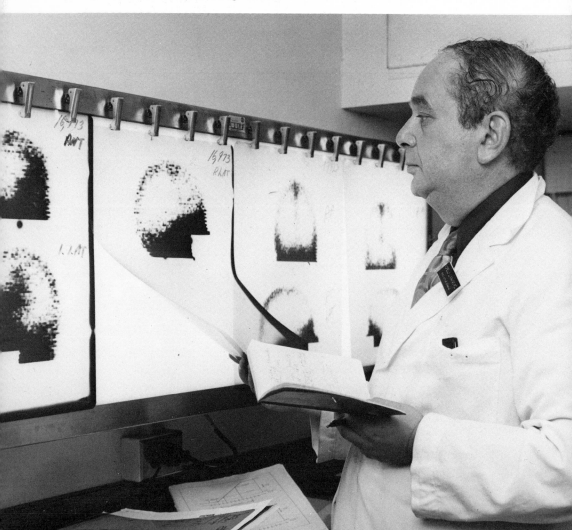

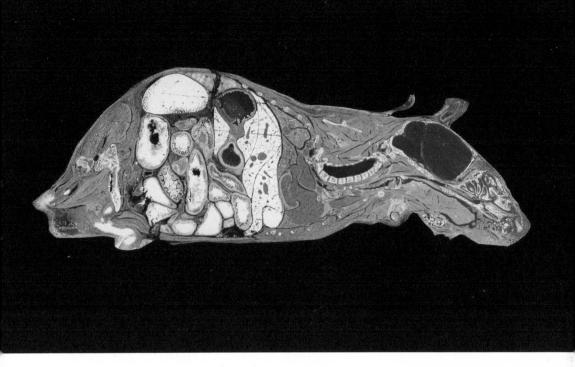

Radioactive water, drunk by a mouse, distributes itself through the body. White areas in the photograph are those that acquired most water.

account for all of them when the job was finished. To avoid the difficulty, he put tiny radioactive sources in each of the tools. Then, when the job was done, a man with a counter could go along the plane and find a misplaced tool by the radiation it was giving off.

The small amount of iodine that enters the body normally collects in the thyroid gland. If the gland becomes cancerous, its cells may move in the bloodstream and start to grow at various points in the body. These abnormal growths are called metastases. When radioactive iodine is administered to a patient, it can serve two purposes. One is to tell whether the gland is functioning as it should. The doctor knows how much iodine he gives to the patient, and the rate at which a Geiger counter clicks when it is held near the gland tells him how much of the iodine is getting to the gland and how fast. From these data he can determine whether the thyroid is functioning in the normal way.

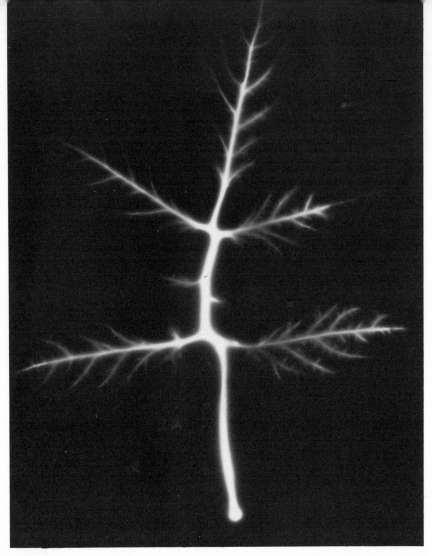

The distribution of radioactive fertilizer in the leaves of a plant is revealed by "radioautographs."

The second purpose is to find the metastases that occur when a thyroid becomes cancerous. The metastases function like the gland they come from and pick up iodine from the system. After giving his patient radioactive iodine, the doctor can run a counter over his body. Where the clicking rate suddenly increases, he knows that a metastasis has started to grow.

A biologist once wanted to know the rate at which water reached various parts of a mouse's body. To find out, he put a radioactive form of hydrogen, the isotope called tritium, into the water and allowed the mouse to drink. After waiting awhile, he killed the mouse and sliced it through the center. Then he exposed the sectioned body to photographic film and developed and printed the film. In the print, white portions showed where the radioactive water had gone. The brain, which exchanges little water with the rest of the system, showed black, and the parts that take up water rapidly (intestines, organs, flesh) were white.

One problem for a student of plants is to find out whether part of a fertilizer actually goes into the plant or simply soaks away into the soil. He wants to know where the fertilizer goes in the plant and how long it takes to go there. He can use radioactive fertilizer. Then, with a Geiger counter held at the leaves,

The leaves are pressed on a photographic plate and allowed to stay in contact while the radioactivity exposes the plate to show early (left) and later (right) distribution.

he can find out how long it takes for the material he is testing to get into that part of the plant.

No matter what the problem, if it involves finding or following something—from atoms to railroad cars—there is probably a way to solve it with radioactive atoms. Almost all elements have usable radioactive isotopes. With ingenuity the engineer or scientist can find one for the job, and its constant, powerful rays acting on the appropriate detector will always show where they are and where they go. Radioisotopes and ways to use them as tracers are among the greatest benefits of the nuclear age.

·(9)·

The Fission Process

Ever since the discovery of radioactivity, just before the beginning of our century, science fiction writers have talked about nuclear energy. They knew that lots of energy was available in the nucleus because bits of energy are released every time a radioactive nucleus disintegrates. Moreover a single nucleus gives up energy not in just one disintegration. It often goes on disintegrating in a dozen steps, giving out energy at each step.

So, the science fiction writers thought, what if you could get together a lot of these nuclei and get them all to give up their stored energy at once? What a tremendous bang you could make in an explosion! What enormous amounts of heat you could have for running engines or heating homes!

But scientists were sure it was all a dream. Nothing they had been able to do had ever changed the slow and deliberate rate at which radioactive nuclei gave up their energy. Indeed there was plenty of energy locked away in the nucleus. But there seemed to be no way to get it. They just had to wait while it dribbled out at its natural rate.

Only a few years before the discovery that changed this whole picture, Lord Rutherford said that ideas of nuclear energy on a grand and useful scale were all "poppycock." How surprised he would have been if he could have lived just a few

Ernest Rutherford of the University of Cambridge was the giant of nuclear research.

years longer! Quite unexpectedly science found a key that unlocked the great store of nuclear energy (often called, rather inaccurately, atomic energy). Suddenly it was possible to put together a vast number of nuclei and, instead of waiting years or thousands of years for them to give up their nuclear energy in little bits and pieces, to command them to give it up much more rapidly and in almost any quantity, even up to the big bang of a nuclear explosion.

86

Enrico Fermi explored the nucleus and constructed the first operating nuclear reactor.

For several years the discovery was missed by the persons who had the evidence. In fact it is one of the ironies of modern physics that Enrico Fermi, one of the greatest physicists of his time, got a Nobel prize for the only wrong bit of physics he ever did.

It happened this way. For many years Fermi and other scientists had observed that if they made neutrons strike uraniun atoms, some peculiar things happened. Fermi studied the situation and found that after the bombardment with neutrons some chemical elements were present that had not been there before. He could tell by chemical tests and by examining the radiation given off that what had been pure uranium at the start contained chemical elements different from uranium after exposure to neutrons. Fermi concluded, quite logically, that the uranium atoms had caught some neutrons and changed into heavier atoms of new elements. Because uranium is the heaviest of the natural atoms, Fermi thought he had made elements not seen before by man—elements we now call the "transuranium elements." (Here the Latin prefix "trans" means "beyond" and "transuranium" means "beyond the uranium atom"—that is, the atoms you come to after following the periodic table from one to 92, and then going beyond: 92, 93, 94 . . .).

What had really happened was discovered a few years later by the German chemists Otto Hahn and Fritz Strassmann. They studied very carefully what went on when uranium was bombarded with neutrons. Their chemical tests found not the transuranium elements Fermi had thought, but elements with atoms about half as heavy as the uranium atoms they started with. They found, for example, barium—element number 56, near the middle of the periodic table.

Otto Frisch, University of Cambridge physicist, has described a walk he took with his aunt, Lise Meitner, in Sweden. She too was a physicist and had been exiled from Nazi Germany where she had been working with Hahn. Frisch and Meitner had heard the news that Hahn and Strassmann had found atoms half as heavy as uranium atoms. They walked and talked, and gradually the explanation came to them. The uranium atoms were not catching neutrons and becoming bigger; they were catching neutrons and splitting in half.

Otto Frisch, a nuclear pioneer, helped his aunt, Lise Meitner, explain fission.

This action was quite different from any nuclear reactions anyone had ever seen before. Nothing bigger than an alpha particle had been known to come out of a nucleus, and most particles that came away in radioactivity were much, much smaller than the alpha particle. But now if barium was formed by splitting, the two parts were more than twenty times as heavy as the alpha particle.

This splitting (or fissioning as it is called by scientists) is indeed what happens when certain isotopes catch neutrons. They

89

Lise Meitner, first in Germany and later in Sweden, studied the fission process.

90

hold the neutrons for a while but become violently unstable as a result. Then they split into nearly equal parts and make new atoms—such as barium, krypton, strontium—about half as heavy as the original atom. When the split occurs, tremendous energy is released; two extremely radioactive atoms are created (like other radioactive atoms, they proceed to change into other atoms), and some free neutrons are released. All of these events have very important consequences.

All of the particles in any nucleus are held inside by strong nuclear forces. When a uranium atom catches a neutron and splits, not only are two smaller nuclei created by the fission, but also the two pieces fly apart at tremendous speeds—in other words, with tremendous amounts of energy. Very quickly the flying pieces strike other atoms around them and slow down and stop. The tremendous energy they started out with is turned into heat. Heat in any substance is the motion of molecules. In solids it is vibration; in gases it is the motion of molecules through space. As a fission fragment leaves the atom from which it comes, it collides with atoms around it, setting them in motion and thereby transferring its energy to heat in the material surrounding it.

Many reactions among atoms release energy. For example, wood, coal, and oil burn to produce heat. The basic chemical reaction is a combination of carbon and hydrogen atoms with atoms of oxygen. The reaction involves only the electrons of the atoms, and no change occurs in their nuclei. But so much more energy comes from the splitting of a uranium atom than from the combination of two atoms in burning as to be almost unbelievable. About a hundred million times as much energy comes from the fission of one uranium atom as from the combination of two atoms during burning. If a ton of coal burned in a furnace would heat a home, the fission in a nuclear reactor of a ton of uranium would heat all the homes in a hundred large cities.

The fission of a uranium atom makes two smaller atoms. The fission does not always occur in the same way; sometimes the two atoms produced (called fission products) are about equal in size. Sometimes one is a lot bigger than the other. Always, though, they are unusually radioactive.

The explanation for the unusual amount of radioactivity is that each of the product atoms has many more neutrons than it ought to have. As one goes through the periodic table from hydrogen at the light-atom end to uranium at the heavy end, the fraction of a stable nucleus made up of neutrons becomes gradually larger, as the ratio of neutrons to protons in the stable nuclei gradually increases. At the light end, stable atoms have equal numbers of protons and neutrons in their nuclei. At the heavy end, on the other hand, nuclei have almost fifteen neutrons for every ten protons. As a result, when a uranium atom captures a neutron and fissions, the new nuclei have many more neutrons that such nuclei would have if they were stable.

To get rid of these extra neutrons, the fission products go through many negative beta decays. At each decay a neutron becomes a proton, and an electron is created and ejected from the nucleus.

The fissioning atom has another way to get rid of extra neutrons. Sometimes when the fission occurs, free neutrons are ejected. These ejected neutrons are the secret of the release of great amounts of nuclear energy.

The reason is that on the average, more than one neutron is ejected for each neutron that is captured in nuclei that fission. In fact, when a uranium nucleus catches a neutron and fissions, on the average two and a half neutrons are released, causing a chain reaction.

Burning is a chain reaction. To make a piece of wood burn, one applies heat to it from a match. The burning produces more heat, and more heat produces more burning.

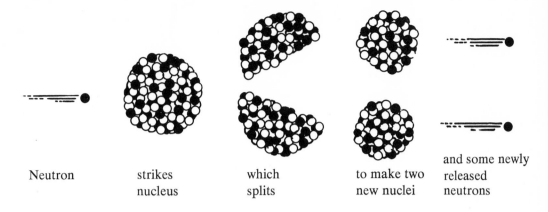

| Neutron | strikes nucleus | which splits | to make two new nuclei | and some newly released neutrons |

In fission a neutron captured by a nucleus causes it to split into two new nuclei of about equal sizes.

Another example of a chain reaction is provided by a set of dominoes stood in a row and made to fall one after another. The falling of one domino produces a push at the next one. The push makes a new fall, and the new fall a new push. In one of these chain reactions the influence that is both cause and effect is heat; in the other it is the falling of the dominoes.

In a nuclear chain reaction, what is required as both cause and effect is free neutrons. A neutron causes an atom to fission. The atom, as it fissions, produces one or more free neutrons. These newly freed neutrons go on to strike more uranium atoms; some of the neutrons are captured, and they cause more fissions, and so on.

Here in this fission process is the energy that is likely to drive motors and light homes in the future when coal and oil supplies run low. In fact it is beginning to do so now. Uranium atoms are brought from mines to a power plant and assembled where they can catch neutrons. Neutrons that are captured cause fission; the fission releases new neutrons to sustain the reaction and heat to drive generators that deliver electric power. Perhaps you are now reading by light that represents energy released in nuclear fission.

And yet it is not easy to produce a chain reaction. If it were easy, the whole earth might have blown up millions of years ago. To make a chain reaction happen, one must get together enough atoms that will fission and then arrange them so that the neutrons freed from one fission can be captured in another nucleus that will also fission. In the next chapter we shall consider the conditions one must set up to make a nuclear chain reaction.

· (10) ·

The Chain Reaction

Of all the isotopes of all the chemical elements—about 1600 all together—only a few experience the special kind of splitting called fission. And of these few only three—uranium-233, uranium-235 and plutonium-239—are useful as nuclear reactor fuels. They undergo the kind of fission that leads to a chain reaction, a fission caused by the capture of a neutron. Because fission always releases neutrons, a chain reaction is possible in a system that contains enough nuclei of this kind. To make such a chain reaction occur, one must put enough of one of these isotopes into an assembly. The whole system must be arranged so that neutrons released by fissions can go on to cause more fissions and release other neutrons before they are lost in some other way.

The fissioning nucleus releases tremendous quantities of energy—millions of times as much as the same amount of material releases when it is burned. This energy in a bomb makes the explosion millions of times as big as that of an ordinary bomb. In an electric generating plant, it offers millions of times as much power as does the same amount of coal or oil.

But there is also a serious drawback in creating heat with nuclear fuel (as we call the fissionable isotope in a chain reaction). As each fission takes place, two atoms smaller than the

95

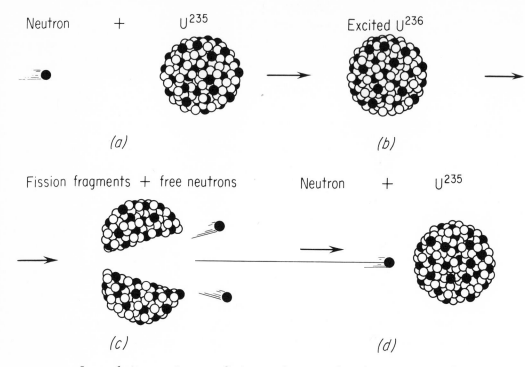

Neutron + U²³⁵ Excited U²³⁶

(a) (b)

Fission fragments + free neutrons Neutron + U²³⁵

(c) (d)

In a chain reaction a splitting nucleus supplies free neutrons that will cause other nuclei to split later.

fissioning atom are created, and they are very radioactive. Thus radioactivity and its radiation, which can be dangerous and inconvenient, are always created by the fissions of a chain reaction. The reactor maker must put shields around the fissioning material to confine the radioactivity.

This difficulty is not the only one he must overcome. In fact, when fission was first understood, scientists were not at all sure that it would be possible to make a chain reaction. Just putting a few fissionable nuclei together is not enough to make the reaction go.

First of all, if only a small number of the fissionable nuclei are present, the neutrons released may hurtle away into space without hitting other fissionable nuclei. Another effect that can prevent chain reaction is capture of neutrons by nuclei that do not fission afterward, and there are many nuclei of that kind. If too many of them are around, they "poison" the reaction by catching and removing the neutrons required to keep the reaction going.

A third difficulty is the speed of the neutrons that come from fission. When they first emerge from the fission they are going very fast, and very fast neutrons are unlikely to get caught by a fissionable nucleus even if they get near it. They are likely to bounce off and keep right on going.

So the engineer who wants to make a nuclear chain reaction must eliminate the difficulties that tend to prevent one. First of all he must get enough usable fuel. Uranium as it comes from a mine is mixed with many other materials, and he must purify it.

Then in his purified uranium he finds that only a tiny fraction—one atom in about 140—is the fissionable isotope uranium-235. Through a difficult process he must separate this U-235 from the other uranium isotopes and collect enough of it.

Next he faces the problem that the neutrons that come from fission are too fast. Some materials such as water and carbon —for example, the graphite of a "lead" pencil—will slow neutrons. Neutrons will bounce off the atoms of such materials and not be captured. At each collision with an atom they lose some speed. After enough collisions they are moving slowly enough to be captured by the fuel nuclei. The process of slowing neutrons is called moderation, and the material used to do it is called a moderator. The moderator is mixed with the fuel or placed around fuel rods.

One more way to encourage the chain reaction is to reduce the number of neutrons that escape from the space in which the fuel is concentrated. After a fuel and moderator mixture is put together in what is called a reactor core, many neutrons can pass out through the surface of the core and get away. To reduce this number, the designer surrounds the core with a neutron reflector. This, too, can be water or graphite. It is some

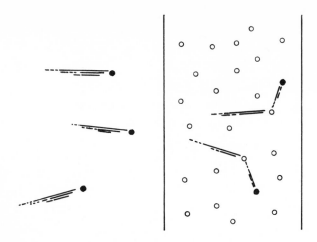

In a moderator like carbon or water, fast neutrons bounce off nuclei and slow down.

material in which escaping neutrons can bounce around and, after several collisions, return to the core.

After fuel, moderator, and reflector are assembled, one big problem remains—controlling the reaction. If it goes too fast, it will overheat the assembly. Fuel will melt, and the system will be damaged. Often people who do not know about nuclear power plants fear that one might explode. As they are constructed, though, explosion is unlikely.

The reactor engineer must provide a means to start and stop the reaction and adjust its rate while it is going on. In the words of reactor design, he must be able to make his reactor subcritical, critical, or supercritical.

A subcritical reactor is one that produces fewer neutrons than it uses up. If too many neutrons escape or are captured in nuclei that will not fission, the neutron population becomes smaller, and chain reaction stops.

The opposite is a supercritical reactor. More neutrons are produced than are used up, and the rate at which the chain reaction occurs increases.

A critical reaction is one in which just one neutron is pro-

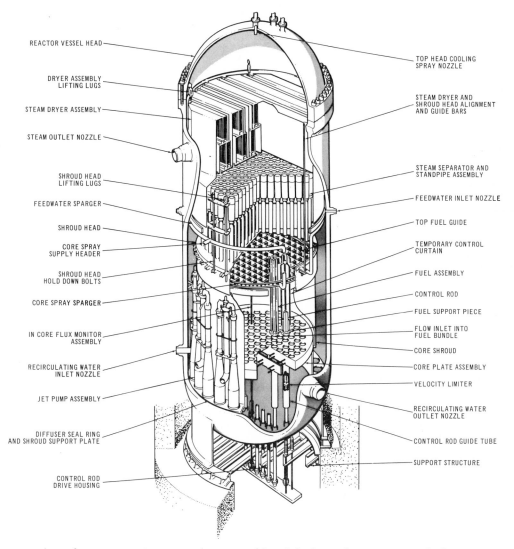

REACTOR VESSEL HEAD

DRYER ASSEMBLY
LIFTING LUGS

STEAM DRYER ASSEMBLY

STEAM OUTLET NOZZLE

SHROUD HEAD
LIFTING LUGS

FEEDWATER SPARGER

SHROUD HEAD

CORE SPRAY
SUPPLY HEADER

SHROUD HEAD
HOLD DOWN BOLTS

CORE SPRAY SPARGER

IN CORE FLUX MONITOR
ASSEMBLY

RECIRCULATING WATER
INLET NOZZLE

JET PUMP ASSEMBLY

DIFFUSER SEAL RING
AND SHROUD SUPPORT PLATE

CONTROL ROD
DRIVE HOUSING

TOP HEAD COOLING
SPRAY NOZZLE

STEAM DRYER AND
SHROUD HEAD ALIGNMENT
AND GUIDE BARS

STEAM SEPARATOR AND
STANDPIPE ASSEMBLY

FEEDWATER INLET NOZZLE

TOP FUEL GUIDE

TEMPORARY CONTROL
CURTAIN

FUEL ASSEMBLY

CONTROL ROD

FUEL SUPPORT PIECE

FLOW INLET INTO
FUEL BUNDLE

CORE SHROUD

CORE PLATE ASSEMBLY

VELOCITY LIMITER

RECIRCULATING WATER
OUTLET NOZZLE

CONTROL ROD GUIDE TUBE

SUPPORT STRUCTURE

A nuclear reactor is a complex assembly of fuel, moderator, control elements, and shielding.

duced for each one that is used up, and the reaction rate stays constant.

You might think of the way people eat as being supercritical, critical and subcritical. When they are children, parents say, "Eat well—you must grow big and strong" (supercritical).

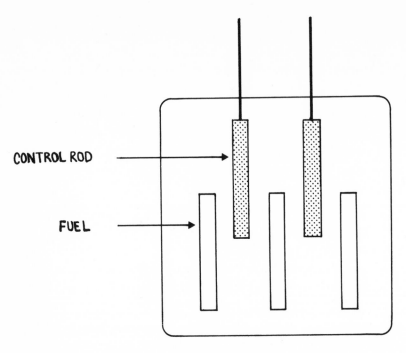

CONTROL ROD

FUEL

Control rods, lowered into a reactor core, catch neutrons to slow the chain reaction.

Then at college age they are big enough; they eat just enough to stay that way (critical). Then, a few years later, if they find they have been eating too much they go on a diet to lose weight by eating less than they use up (subcritical).

At least four ways are available to control a reactor. One is to add and subtract fuel. If part of the fuel can be pushed in or pulled out of the core, the reactor can be made to start, stop, speed up, and slow down.

A second way is to move parts of the reflector. Pulling away reflecting material allows more neutrons to escape and causes the reaction to slow down and stop.

A third way is to add and subtract moderator. For example, if the moderator is water, the operator can make more water flow into the core or flow away from it. When too little moderator is available, neutrons that ought to slow down and then hit fuel nuclei continue instead to move too fast until they reach the edge of the core and escape.

But the most common way is insertion and withdrawal of neu-tron-absorbing control rods. The designer puts into the rod a material that readily captures neutrons; it soaks them up like a blotter. Boron, for example, is such a material. Pushing the rod into the core causes neutrons to disappear and the reaction to slow down. Pulling it out allows the neutron population and the reaction rate to increase.

After the problems of making a reactor are solved and the chain reaction is made to go, other matters must be taken care of if the reactor is to continue to operate safely. One is shield-ing. Men and materials near the reactor must be safe from the huge amounts of radiation pouring from fission products—those atoms that are made each time a fuel atom fissions. Heavy shields of concrete, steel, water, and such materials are designed to keep this radiation from escaping.

Heavy shielding contains reactor radiation.

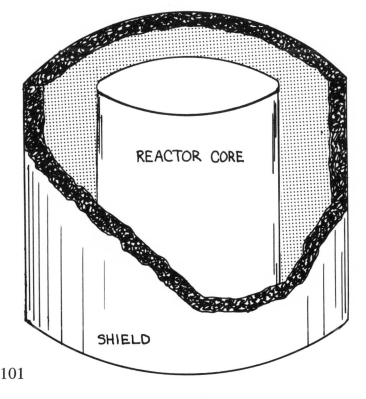

REACTOR CORE

SHIELD

Another concern is heat. The chain reaction generates much of it, and if all of it stayed in the reactor, the temperature would continue to rise until something melted. Moreover many reactors are built to provide heat for power plants, and the designer must get the heat out of the reactor core to the place where he wants to use it.

Cooling is accomplished in the same way that a steam or hot-water system takes heat from a furnace in the cellar and distributes it to radiators throughout the house. Some fluid passes through the reactor core. It may be a gas like carbon dioxide or steam. It may be a liquid like water, mercury, or even liquid sodium. In going through the core, which is very hot, the fluid heats up itself. Then it flows away to a cooler place—for example, a steam boiler—where it loses its heat and cools down.

Fluid flowing through the core removes heat.

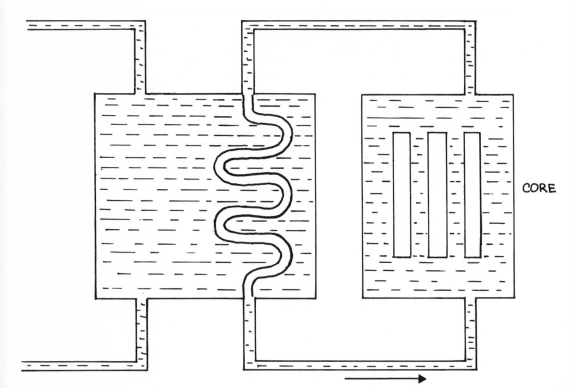

CORE

Finally it flows back into the core again to get more heat and go through the process all over again.

Another question the reactor operator must answer is how to provide fresh fuel. In view of the great amount of energy available from a tiny amount of uranium, it is strange that he cannot just put in enough fuel for a reactor lifetime.

But one difficulty prevents this kind of operation. Of the new atoms produced in fission, many are reactor poisons. They capture the neutrons that are required to keep the reaction going. Thus only a small fraction of the fuel atoms—two or three in every hundred—can be made to fission. Then the poisons become too great, and the reaction would slow down and stop if they were not removed. The operator must remove the fuel, chemically remove the poisons, purify the fuel, and add some new fuel to make up for what has been used. Then the new fuel rods can be inserted into the reactor.

Indeed, the engineers who design and operate reactors do not find it easy to do so. To make a reactor they must prepare fuel, insert moderator, provide control, build shielding, and remove the heat. As the reactor operates, they must repeatedly remove and reprocess fuel. For their efforts, though, they get huge sources of smokeless energy capable of providing huge quantities of electric power.

·(11)·

Nuclear Fusion

The largest nuclei all give up energy in radioactivity, by firing out fast particles and gamma rays and changing into smaller nuclei. A few of them also give up energy in fission. They usually split into two nearly equal pieces that separate at great speed and heat the material around them as they hit it.

It would be logical—but wrong—to think that any process that makes a nucleus smaller would release energy as a stone loses energy in rolling down a hill. Matters do not work out that way. If anybody could gradually make a nucleus into smaller pieces—say by taking away a piece at a time or by repeatedly cutting it in two—he would be getting energy in the process only down to nuclear sizes of about fifty or sixty particles. To make nuclei still smaller, he would have to supply energy each time he cut or subtracted—just as he would have to supply energy to take the stone back up the hill.

We can also look at the process in the opposite direction. Two of the smallest nuclei can be made to collide and join together to make a single larger nucleus. Scientists say that they fuse, just as two drops of mercury will fuse if they are pushed together. In the process of fusion the two nuclei always expel one or two particles (often a proton), and these emitted particles come away very fast. In others words, they carry away

104

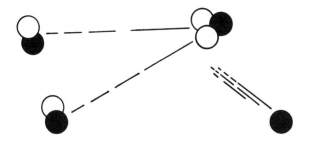

Two small nuclei fuse to make a new one, plus a free neutron.

great quantities of energy—much more than is needed to make the two nuclei fuse.

An engineer would hope to use this energy. He might make the emitted particles strike his apparatus and heat it. Heat, after all, is just molecules in motion, and if the motion of an expelled proton can be transferred to the wall of a boiler by making the particle collide with the wall, the boiler will heat up. It will then produce steam, and the steam could drive a power plant.

It might also be possible to make the expelled proton enter a magnetic field near a coil of wire. The force between the proton and the magnetic field could make a current flow in the wire, and current flowing in a wire is electric power.

For reasons like these, man hopes he will one day generate usable power with this process that he calls nuclear fusion.

No one so far has made a fusion reactor that can do this job—that is, make power by causing the fusion of small nuclei. But as with fission reactors, there is good reason to try to make one. As with fission, the amount of energy one would make from each pound of fuel would be enormous. The reason, once again, is that the reaction works with nuclear forces that are millions of times as great as the chemical forces involved in burning gas, oil, and coal.

105

Another advantage of a fusion reactor would be cheapness of its fuel. Uranium, which a fission reactor consumes, is rare and expensive to get. But a fusion reactor would use elements like hydrogen, helium, and lithium. The reactor designer can get all he needs quite easily from sea water, the surface of the earth, and its atmosphere.

A third advantage would be lack of contamination. After a fission reactor has operated for a while, it has made large quantities of dangerously radioactive fission products. They must be safely contained so that their radiation will not damage plants, animals, or men. A fusion reactor would not create much, if any, radioactive contamination. The atoms it produced would all be at the low end of the periodic table where little radioactivity exists. They would not have the great excess of neutrons that make fission products highly radioactive.

But wishing for a fusion reactor will not make one. The task is hard. In simplest terms, what one has to do is push two nuclei together until their nuclear forces take hold and they fuse to make a single nucleus. The two nuclei have positive charges, and they push each other away with a mighty repulsion.

The only way anybody can see to do the job, with the large numbers of nuclei one must have to get worth-while amounts of power, is to push lots of them together at tremendous temperatures. In a gas such as one might make up by mixing hydrogen and helium isotopes, high temperature means that all of the atoms and molecules are moving at great speeds. You could imagine them as a great room with lots of fast-moving ping-pong balls in it, all of them bouncing off each other and off the walls.

The temperatures one would have to have would be almost unbelievable—much hotter than a candle flame or a welder's torch or even the spark it makes in arc welding. The mixture will have to be so hot that electrons are stripped from their atoms and the mixture becomes a mixture of electrons, ionized atoms that have lost one or more electrons, and bare nuclei

106

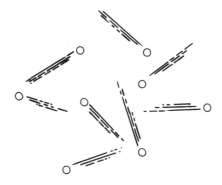

In a gas at high temperature, molecules are moving with great speeds.

from which all electrons have been stripped. Such a mixture is called a plasma.

In such a plasma, fast-moving nuclei might be crowded close enough together that a large number would collide and fuse. The energy produced could be used to make electric power.

Such a plasma looks like the glowing gas column that lights up a neon sign. But it is much hotter than such a neon discharge. Its temperature is many millions of degrees, like that of the center of the sun.

The plasma is, in fact, so hot that no material can contain it. Any material that was heated to the temperature of a plasma would melt and become a plasma itself.

Despite the difficulties of making a container, one problem of the fusion-reactor maker is to make a plasma that is dense. He must crowd the plasma into a small volume so that nuclei will collide with other nuclei and fuse. Because metal and glass containers would either melt or make the plasma too cool to do its work, he must hope to contain his plasma with electric and magnetic forces.

Even when he does this, he faces great difficulties. The plasma, like the glowing gas you can watch in a neon sign, turns and twists and tries to escape.

But man continues to hope he can make a fusion power plant, because he knows fusion reactors exist. One of them is our sun.

107

The sun, like other suns you see at night and call stars, is a huge ball of plasma held together by gravity. The source of its energy was long a mystery to men. Then a few years ago Hans Bethe, a Cornell University physicist, explained the sun's energy. It comes from a complicated series of nuclear reactions. The net result of these reactions is that four hydrogen nuclei (protons) fuse to make one helium nucleus (two protons, two neutrons) and a great amount of excess energy. In the process two positive electrons are emitted.

The hydrogen bomb is a man-made fusion reactor. Its great pressure and temperature, produced by exploding a fission bomb at the center, cause hydrogen nuclei to fuse and release their energy.

Considering all of these facts together, we can see that man has good reason to try to build a fusion reactor but that he has a tremendous scientific job to do before he is able to make one. The incentive for the task is the great amount of power he can get from cheap fuels that do not produce ashes or radioactive wastes. The difficulty is that he cannot make a reactor as big as the sun or use a hydrogen bomb explosion every time he wants to generate power. Because of these incentives and difficulties many scientists in many countries are hard at work on this problem of "taming the H bomb." They think they know fairly well how the problem is to be solved.

The fusion scientists know their fuel will be isotopes of hydrogen, helium, and lithium. Their containment will be provided by electric and magnetic fields. By combining these isotopes and fields in devices of various shapes and sizes, they are coming gradually closer to an operative fusion machine. With enough study and experimentation, they will probably make a working power plant.

To see what fuel the plant must use, physicists study the collisions of nuclei of hydrogen-1, -2, and -3, helium-3 and -4, and lithium-6. One way to study them is to use a particle accelerator. They can make a beam of fast protons and aim it at something that has a lot of hydrogen—water, for example. By observing the results, they can see what happens when a proton in the beam strikes a proton in the nucleus of a hydrogen atom. With such studies they learn what happens when any pair of these isotopes collide at any speed, how likely the two nuclei are to fuse, what particles are produced, and how much energy is released. From all this knowledge they can predict what happens in a plasma made of any mixture of the isotopes.

They also study plasma containment. When an electric current flows, it makes a magnetic field. When a plasma particle moves in a magnetic field, the field exerts a force on the particle, making it move in a circle. The hope is to wind coils of wire and put current through them (and also through the plasma itself) in such a way that the magnetic and electric fields produced will hold the twisting, writhing plasma—at least long enough to make it give up a share of its energy.

One plasma device—a cylinder with a discharge through a column of gas.

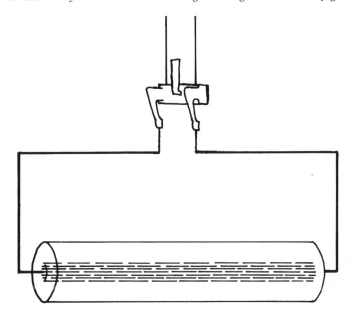

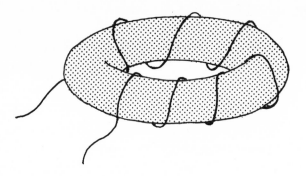

A doughnut-shaped container surrounded by coils. Currents in the coils can make a plasma in the tube.

Many shapes and sizes of coils and containments have been tried already. For example, one can make a plasma in a long, straight glass tube and then make a huge electric current flow right along the tube in the plasma. The magnetic field that is formed will suddenly constrict the plasma into a thin narrow line down the middle of the tube. One can also make a doughnut-shaped tube and wind electric coils around the doughnut.

Some devices with which scientists try to make and to hold plasmas operate steadily like furnaces fueled by oil and coal. Some, though, work in a series of small pulses or explosions like bombs going off. Their reasoning is that plasma does not have to be confined for very long. In some experimental machines the plasma is contained for as short a time as a thousandth of a second.

In a device of this kind, a long and complicated series of actions can take place in the short time it takes to make a single explosion-like pulse with the machine. For example, the machine can let a small amount of hydrogen gas into a vacuum. A burst of current through the tube makes the gas into a plasma. Then the plasma is compressed by a surge of current through a coil. The plasma is moved from one place to another by currents in other coils. All this is accomplished within a thousandth of a second.

Of course the sequence of operations is controlled with electronic apparatus, and the measurements are automatically re-

 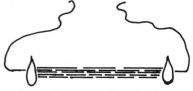

The plasma sequence: let in gas; *make a plasma with a discharge;*

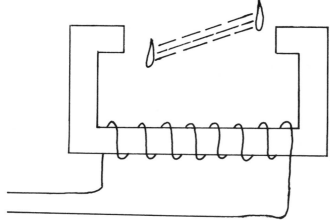

shape and move it with magnetic fields.

corded on meters and charts. And if you watch it all happen, you only see a big flash and hear an explosion.

Fusion efforts have been going on for about twenty years, and yet no one has made a successful power reactor. A "successful" fusion reactor would make more power than is required to operate it.

But we have some signs of success. The quantity a fusion engineer measures to see how well he is doing is called the time-density product. Time refers to the period during which he can hold the plasma together before instability makes it blow itself apart. Density is a measure of how many particles—ions and the electrons stripped from them—he can crowd into his containment space. The engineer knows about what number he must get when he multiplies the density and the time together if his reactor is to be successful.

The fusion experts have been trying many methods. After experimenting with one machine for a long time, trying different shapes and sizes of coils and short and long pulses, they make a new machine and try again. Always they use what they learn

111

from one set of experiments to make the next attempt better than the last one.

The sign of their success is that the number they get by multiplying containment time by plasma density has been gradually increasing. Sometimes one group of experimenters working with one kind of system can show the best result, and sometimes it is another group with another system. But the best value that any group can get becomes gradually better. One scientist has estimated that the best value anybody can get for this product improves by a factor of ten about every two years. That is, on the average it is ten times as good after two years as it was at the beginning of the two-year period.

The future of fusion is hard to predict with real accuracy. Dr. Robert Hirsch, assistant director of research for the United States fusion effort, has recently put it this way: research now going on might show by 1978 whether a fusion reactor is really possible. If it turns out that one is possible, we might hope to see a working power plant within seven or eight years after that. With the best of luck, then, a nuclear-fusion power industry may attain significant size before the end of this century.

· (12) ·

Discovery and Exploration

We contemplate the nucleus with wonder, first because we can know so much about anything so incredibly small and second because all that we know about it has been learned in so incredibly short a time. This tiny heart of the atom is so small that if we could line up a billion of them side by side, the line they would make would only reach across a pin prick. Yet we know not only that it exists but also what makes it up and how the pieces are arranged.

And so short a time has passed since the nucleus was discovered! The earth, this planet we live on, has existed for about five billion years. Of that time man has inhabited the earth for about a million years. History as we know it—that part of man's lifetime for which we can find some written record—goes back five or six thousand years. Although some men guessed long, long ago that the atom should exist, we have actually known the atom for less than a century, and the nucleus was discovered only in 1911. All that we know of this tiny core of the atom we have had to find out in a mere tick of time.

Most people admire a graceful building such as a Gothic cathedral or the great domed capitol building in Washington. To men who study the nucleus, this little object has the same kind of beauty. Like an arch or a splendid round window, it has its own

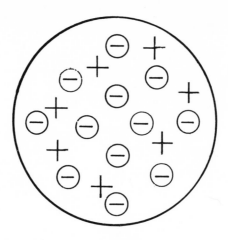

An early model of the atom as a positive pudding with electrons stuck in like raisins.

arrangement of parts, its own pattern. Like the artist, the nuclear scientist must be clever, imaginative, skillful, and devoted.

Such a man was Ernest Rutherford, later Lord Rutherford, who discovered the nucleus in 1911. Even before he discovered it, he had learned a lot about the atom. He had observed the radiations that came from radioactivity and found out how they acted when they struck things. Later, when he knew there was a nucleus, he could tell that much of what he knew actually concerned the nucleus, not the whole atom.

When Rutherford came upon the atom, the electron and proton had been discovered. Then came the discovery, in 1898, of the radiations from radioactivity. Rutherford and his colleagues proceeded to find out much about alpha, beta, and gamma radiation from radioactive atoms.

What they knew about alpha particles led to discovery of the nucleus. Knowing what they did of the atom, the men of Rutherford's time made up their model of the atom as a pudding

114

of positive charge with the negative electrons embedded in it like raisins.

Then two of Rutherford's students tried the famous experiment with gold foil that he suggested to them, and from their results Rutherford concluded that something in the atom was much harder and heavier than pudding. It was, of course, the atomic nucleus, and we have been studying it ever since the experiment showed that it existed.

Not that we have studied only the nucleus as the result of the discovery. The fact that the atom had a nucleus inspired Niels Bohr to study the behavior of the electrons, which, he knew, must make up the outer layers. Bohr, a Danish physicist, was the great man of the atom as Rutherford was the great man of the nucleus. Within two years of Rutherford's discovery of the nucleus, Bohr made the first big step toward an understanding of the atomic electrons and how they are arranged.

Meanwhile, of course, others tried to understand the nucleus. At first they were misled because they knew only two particles, electrons and protons. Knowing the mass and charge of a nucleus, they tried to imagine how it could be made of enough protons to produce its mass and enough electrons to give it the proper charge.

Such a nucleus was mainly a lump in the middle of the atom. No one had any useful ideas about how things were arranged inside or why nuclei behaved as they did. For example, they had no explanation of radioactivity. Then in 1928 George Gamow, working in Europe, and Ronald Gurney and Edward Condon, studying the nucleus in the United States, compared the energies of alpha particles and gamma rays and the half-lives of nuclei. That is, they considered how fast the alpha particles came out and how much matter the gamma rays of different atoms would go through. They compared these energies with each other, and they compared them with the time it took for the atoms they

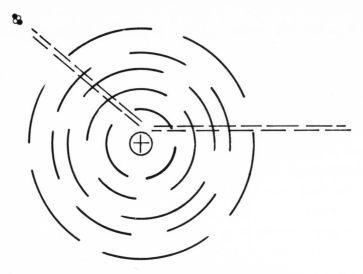

A tiny positively charged nucleus scatters alpha particles.

came from to disappear from a sample by changing into other atoms. They found that with the right equations and the right kind of calculations they could find one energy from another and the half-lives from the energies. The study of nuclear structure had begun.

The study took a long step forward when James Chadwick, who worked with Rutherford, discovered the neutron in 1932. It showed up as a radiation that occurred when certain substances were bombarded with other particles, and this new radiation went much farther into matter than any other kind. What happens is that protons bombarding certain atoms knock neutrons out of them. The neutrons, having no charge, are not held back by the electric forces that stop such particles as alpha particles; each one goes right on until it makes a head-on collision with a nucleus that captures it. Thus they can go a long, long way.

Knowing about the neutron, physicists could make better guesses about how nuclei are constructed. In fact they knew almost all about them when the discovery of fission in 1939

116

gave them all a big surprise. Here was a brand new phenomenon not at all to be expected from such matters as radioactivity, half-lives and nuclear sizes. It was, of course, a history-making discovery. Shortly afterward, for better or for worse, the world had an atom bomb and nuclear power plants.

Of course ever since the discovery of the nucleus, scientists had been finding out all that they could about all of the nuclei. They made great charts and filled books with tables of numbers. So by the time that the atom bomb was exploded, they could see the possibility of a hydrogen bomb and nuclear fusion. Their many studies had told them how much energy every nucleus had in it, and they could tell that by making two of the small nuclei fuse, they could take out more energy than they must put in. Moreover their experiments with giant atom smashers told them how likely it was that any particular pair of nuclei would fuse if they bumped into each other hard enough. From all of this information they could work out the conditions under which a fusion power plant might operate.

Many years after Rutherford, scattering experiments continue to explore the nucleus and its pieces.

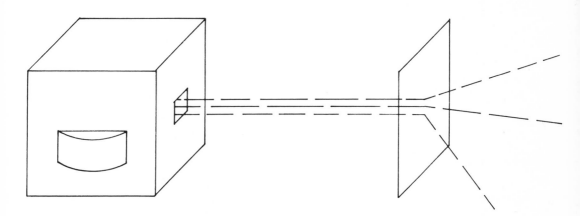

Many more experiments with nuclei have taught men the fine details of structure, and many experiments are still going on. Even so many years after Rutherford, these experiments are much like his. Beams of particles are scattered from various kinds of atoms, and the ways that they bounce off are used as indications of the structure of nuclei and the particles in them. Instead of the radioactive source that Rutherford used, experimenters now produce intense beams of many kinds of particles with huge machines, and they use automatic counters and great computers instead of squinting through microscopes and counting little flashes of light as Rutherford had to do. Yet the experiments of today are really just more elaborate versions of the one he did in 1911.

The men and women who make nuclear experiments today can determine the different arrangements in which any nucleus can exist, the different amounts of energy it can contain in different arrangements, the energy of the gamma rays that are given off when the nucleus shifts from one arrangement to another, and many other details that fill books of nuclear data.

Although measurements remain to be made and problems remain to be solved, it is almost fair to say that the nucleus is understood. Fusion power remains a task not yet accomplished, but it is not really a nuclear problem. The nuclear physics involved has all been explored. The part that remains to be done is properly classified among other branches of physics and engineering.

The knowledge of nuclear structure has led to the study of the structure of the fundamental particles. In 1911 the newly found nucleus was a lump of positive something, and nobody knew its makeup. Now the proton, neutron, and electron are similar lumps of something. So too are other particles that science finds it can manufacture by bumping these atomic particles together hard enough. So we start out on the next stage of the journey and look for the nature of tiny particles as a few years ago we started out to find the nature of the nucleus. We hope, of course, that the next century will teach us about the tiny particles as the last century has taught about the atom and its parts. We hope too that with knowledge will come wisdom. We hope that minds sharpened on the problems of the nucleus and its particles will deal well with problems of the world that they make up and the men who live in it.

Glossary

alpha particles: A particularly stable combination of two protons and two neutrons, identical with the helium-4 nucleus.

annihilate: To make into nothing. Specifically, when a particle and its antiparticle (for example, electron and positron) meet and destroy each other, leaving nothing but electromagnetic radiation.

antiparticle: A particle having a mass that is the same as, but a charge that is opposite to, that of another particle.

atom: The smallest bit of any chemical element, consisting of a nucleus and electrons around it.

beta particle: A fast electron or positron emitted in the disintegration of a radioactive nucleus.

chain reaction: Any reaction sustained because the product, or effect, is the same as the cause. Specifically the nuclear chain reaction, in which neutrons are the initiating agent and neutrons are also produced by the reaction, which is fission.

charge: A quantity of electricity.

closed shell: In the outer layers of an atom, a set of electrons in which all spaces are filled.

control rod: A rod containing material that absorbs neutrons. It is inserted into the core of a reactor to reduce the reaction rate.

120

Glossary

counter: a device that detects radiation and counts the number of particles or photons falling on it.

critical: (Of nuclear reactor.) Producing free neutrons exactly as fast as they are disappearing from the reaction volume.

daughter: The atom that is made by radioactive disintegration of another atom, which is called the "parent."

detector: A sensitive device that produces a signal when it is struck by a photon or particle from a radioactive atom that disintegrates.

disintegration: The process in which a radioactive nucleus gives off radiation and changes into another form.

electron: One of the three kinds of particles that make up atoms. It has a negative charge equal to the charge of the proton and a mass $1/1800$ that of the proton.

element: A substance in which all atoms have the same number of protons, such as hydrogen, helium, oxygen, and carbon. Elements are to be distinguished from compounds, like water and salt, in which the smallest pieces are molecules made up of two or more atoms of different kinds.

fission: The process in which a large nucleus splits into two roughly equal parts.

fission product: Any of the new atoms made by fission.

force: An influence tending to move a body, such as a push or pull.

fuel: The nuclear material in which fissions take place to sustain a nuclear chain reaction.

fusion: The process in which the nuclei of two small atoms join to make one large nucleus, releasing energy as they do so.

gamma photon: A bundle of electromagnetic radiation released in a radioactive disintegration.

gamma ray: A phrase often used for a gamma photon. It can also mean many gamma photons following the same path.

Geiger counter: A particular kind of detector consisting of a gas-filled tube in which an electrical discharge occurs if it is

121

triggered by a particle or photon from a radioactive disintegration.

ground state: That arrangement of the electrons in an atom in which they have the lowest energy and are therefore most stable.

half-life: The time required for half of the atoms in a radioactive specimen to disintegrate.

ion: An atom that has more electrons or fewer electrons than its normal number, the normal number being equal to the number of protons in the nucleus. Also a molecule that has more or fewer electrons than the number of protons in all of its nuclei.

ionizing: (Of radiation.) Energetic enough to form ions in the material through which it passes.

isotope: Two atoms are isotopes of the same element if they have equal numbers of protons in the nucleus but different numbers of neutrons.

mass: That property of anything that makes it resist acceleration. It is a measure of the amount of material in the body.

model: A form of anything physical that is imagined for purposes of description or calculation. One makes a model by saying, "Now suppose the atom looked like this; then . . ."

moderator: A substance put into a nuclear reactor core so that neutrons will bounce from its atoms and slow down.

molecule: A combination of two or more atoms making up the smallest bits of a chemical compound, such as water and salt.

negative charge: One of the two kinds of electric charge, the other being "positive."

neutron: One of the three kinds of particles that make up atoms. This one has no electric charge and has slightly more mass than the proton.

nuclear reactor: An assembly in which a nuclear chain reaction is caused to take place.

Glossary

nucleus: The tiny, dense, positively charged object that forms the center of an atom.

parent: The radioactive nucleus that disintegrates to make a different kind of nucleus, which is called the "daughter."

particle: A bit of matter so small that it cannot be separated into smaller pieces, although the alpha particle is exceptional, being composed of four smaller particles.

periodic table: A listing of the chemical elements by the sizes of their atoms in such a way that elements having similar properties fall together and properties repeat according to a recognizable pattern as one proceeds from lighter to heavier atoms.

plasma: Matter so hot that electrons are stripped from nuclei and complete atoms and molecules no longer exist (or exist only in small numbers).

positron: The antiparticle of the electron. It has the same mass as the electron but a charge that is positive whereas the electron charge is negative.

proton: One of the three particles making up atoms. It has a positive charge equal in magnitude to the charge of the electron and a mass that is 1800 times that of the electron and a bit smaller than that of the neutron.

radiation: Fast particles and electromagnetic photons emitted from radioactive nuclei during radioactive disintegration.

radioactive: (Of an atom.) Capable of disintegrating and emitting radiation. (Of a substance.) Containing radioactive atoms that are disintegrating and emitting radiation.

reactor: (See nuclear reactor.)

reflector: A substance placed around a nuclear reactor core with the purpose of making neutrons leaving the core turn back and re-enter the core.

shell: A set of positions that can be occupied by electrons around the nucleus of an atom.

123

Glossary

shielding: Material placed around a nuclear reactor core or radioactive material to prevent radiation from escaping.

stable: Not likely to change.

stability curve: In a chart of the nuclides (different kinds of nuclei), a line that runs through the most stable isotope of each chemical element.

state: A particular position and shape in which an electron (or other particle) can come to rest. Also, a collection of such positions and shapes that can be occupied by an equal number of particles.

tracer: A group of radioactive atoms used for the purpose of determining the position or movement of any body or substance by means of the radiation given off.

transuranium elements: Those elements with atoms that are heavier than uranium atoms. Such atoms do not exist in nature and must be man-made.

Index

125

Index